LIVING IN THE U.S.A.

Living in the U.S.A.

ALISON RAYMOND LANIER

CHARLES SCRIBNER'S SONS   New York

217293

To all my known and unknown friends
throughout our shrinking world . . .

Table of Contents

Dear Reader,

Hundreds of people from all over the world helped with the writing of this book over a period of many years. During its final preparation, however, a few provided extra help.

My grateful thanks go to *Mrs. Warren Wheeler* who carefully read and helpfully criticized the chapters as they appeared; *Mr. Bryant Wedge,* Director of the Institute for the Study of National Behavior, who helped to stimulate and clarify my thinking about this country's ideas; *Mr. Ernest A. Smith,* professor of sociology at Hunter College, who contributed to the chapter on "Teen-Age Dating," as did *Miss Gwen Harper,* Program Director of the Camp Fire Girls; *Mrs. James Stretch,* an American returned from overseas who shed new light on American manners and contributed helpfully to the chapter on schools.

During the whole process, *Mrs. Ralph Evers* maintained a cheery smile, no matter how often chapters had to be reworked!

Lastly, I am ever grateful to my enthusiastic and understanding husband who not only takes less-than-perfect housekeeping in his stride, but also, with unfailing grace, lets me try out ideas with him at any hour!

ALISON R. LANIER

SPECIAL NOTE TO READERS FROM CANADA, MEXICO, CENTRAL AND SOUTH AMERICA

To fellow Americans from other parts of the hemisphere—my apologies!

Throughout this book I have used the word "American" many times to mean "of the United States," with the full knowledge that the United States is only a *part* of the Americas. The trouble is that we have an unwieldy and difficult name to use! It is cumbersome to xiv   **Living in the U.S.A.**

keep saying "North American," and in any case this includes Mexico and Canada too. It is impossible to say "United Statesian"! So please forgive my inaccurate and not necessarily inclusive use of the word "American." It is done through no lack of appreciation or awareness of all the many customs, cultures, and countries that are equally American.

LIVING IN THE U.S.A.

Part I

FOR ALL VISITORS—SHORT OR LONG TERM

First Impressions

Jet airplanes circle the world; news is "bounced off" satellites so that we literally "see" each other more and more clearly in our homes and varied lands. Naturally such developments lead to increasing business among nations. With this comes the transfer of families—negotiators, salesmen, heads of companies—and with each there is usually a wife. Often there are children, brothers, grandmothers as well.

Transfer to the United States is often a difficult transition. Things move fast, spaces are great, variations are confusing, Americans speak with many tongues. The position of children, teenagers, and old people in American social patterns is often unexpected to others. The daily mechanics of living are bewildering. Why must one have insurance? What about household help? What are the pitfalls in buying a car? What kinds of taxes must be paid? When? What customs and courtesies are different?

PACE

For many people the pace of life is what is most confusing, especially at the beginning. One's first impression is likely to be that everyone is in a rush—often under pressure. City people appear always to be hurrying to get where they are going, waiting impatiently to be served a meal, restlessly seeking attention in a store, elbowing others as they try to complete their errands. At first this may appear rude. Bus drivers will be abrupt, waiters will hurry you, people will push past you. You will miss smiles, brief conversations with strangers, small courtesies. Don't take it personally. The pace

5

is gentler outside the big cities, as it is in other countries as well.

Americans who live in cities assume that everyone is equally competitive and self-sufficient; they expect others to "push back" just as city people do in Tokyo or Paris, in Beirut or São Paulo. But the minute they discover you are a stranger, most Americans become quite kindly and will take great trouble to help you. Many of them first came to the city as strangers and they remember how frightening a new city can be. If you need assistance or want to ask a question, choose a nice-looking person and say:

"I am a stranger here. Can you help me?"

Most people will stop, smile at you, and help you find your way, or advise you in whatever is needed. *But you must let them know that you need help;* otherwise they will pass you unseeing and unheeding, wrapped in their own concerns. A few may not respond helpfully. If this happens, don't be discouraged; just ask someone else. Most Americans enjoy helping a stranger.

PEOPLE

Who are these people who are swirling around you? Some 204 million of them now call America "home," but in fact they have their origins in every part of the world. The names you see over shop doors tell you so, as do the varied types of faces you pass on the streets. A roll call of school children will include such names as: Adams, Ali, Bykowski, Capparella, Fujita, Gonzales, Mukerji, Nusseibeh, and Wong. Mostly these diverse backgrounds have not been blended in the so-called American "melting pot." In fact the idea that America is a melting pot is largely a myth. What exists more often is a kind of side-by-side living in which ethnic groups retain many of their own customs and social traditions. They merge into the American stream only in certain aspects of life—in schools, sports, business, and science, to name a few—but keep to many of their own customs and patterns socially and at home. Many tensions now apparent in American life stem from the interplay of varied cultures on each other. The plus side of this situation is the richness that comes with variety; the wide freedom of choice that exists in ideas and dress, in food and customs. The minus side is that unseen barriers do still exist for some people, most often in the worlds of business and housing—particularly at lower income levels. Nonetheless, everyone can find his own familiar world here —be it in spices or fruits, churches or national groups, newspapers or music.

INFORMALITY

Although American informality is well known, many interpret it as a "lack of respect" when they first encounter it, especially in the business world. The almost immediate use of first names, for example, jars on nerves long accustomed to deference or respect from men of lower rank.

Don't be surprised if Americans do not shake hands. They often just nod or smile instead. A casual "Hi" or "How are you doing?" or "Hello" often takes the place of a formal handshake, but it means the same thing. Nor will you find Americans circulating about a group in the office or at a party giving each one a personal farewell. Instead—again the different sense of timing and pace— they will just wave a cheery "good-by" or say something informal to the whole group such as "Well, see you tomorrow" or "So long everybody." Then they will disappear. No handshakes.

Often you will see men working at office desks in shirt-sleeves, sometimes without their ties. They may lean far back in their chairs and even put their feet on the radiator or desk while they talk on the telephone. This also is not meant to be rude. Once we get out of the tense, hurried city streets, we are a loose-jointed, informal, re-laxed people.

Our pace is total—either totally hurried, intense, work-absorbed, and competitive (in play as well as work); or else totally at ease, re-laxed, "undone," and informal, our feet up, our manner breezy. We tend to swing between these extremes. This is the pendulum you need to understand if you are to understand America and its people.

Chapter 2

Customs Vary with Cultures

Many American customs will catch you offguard; the same thing happens to us when we visit another country. People living in varied cultures handle many small daily things differently. What a dull world it would be if this were not true!

Some differences are minor, and one soon becomes accustomed to them. At first, for example, Asian women may be startled at having their hair washed and dressed by men; visitors may be amazed to see men wearing wigs; people may find the transitory quality of much American life odd—the fact, for example, that one can rent art by the week or the entire furnishings of an apartment, from sofa and beds to the last spoon, on less than eight hours' notice. "Packaged" living is part of today's American scene, part of its transient mobility and pace.

At the same time—and perhaps even *because* of this sense of impermanence—houses interest Americans greatly. They spend much time thinking and reading and talking about the design of houses, their decorations, how to improve them. Many weekend hours are passed in "do-it-yourself" projects around the home. People love to inspect each other's houses. Since they would thoroughly enjoy visiting and examining a house in another country, they assume that you will probably have the same desire. Don't be surprised, therefore, if you are shown the entire house from top to bottom, including bathrooms and closets! Americans think they are doing you a favor. Don't make the mistake of refusing; the whole house may have been especially tidied up for you!

MOTION

The constant restless motion of Americans may be startling at first. People in the flat Middle West think nothing of driving 75 to 100 miles just to have dinner with a friend; they go to a far-off city for an evening of theater or music or even a movie. Countless young people select a college thousands of miles away from their families "just to see another part of the country." Barely in their teens, they go off in droves to see what lies back of beyond.

OUR IGNORANCE

You may come upon Americans who are incredibly ignorant about your country. If so, be patient with them. Unfortunately, we do not teach enough about other cultures, customs, or even geography in our schools; we have always been so insulated by oceans that we are not readily exposed to different cultures and other ways of doing things. If Americans crudely try to help you with something that has long been totally familiar to you, if they comment on your good English when you have spoken it all your life, if they confuse your country with another thousands of miles away, be patient with their ignorance. This huge continent has been developed from a primeval and virgin land into the modern dynamo that it now is in a remarkably short time—about 300 years. We have been absorbed with our own growth, with road building, city building, free education for millions of children, the assimilation of countless strangers; with the inventions, discoveries, and developments that our science and technology have contributed to the world. Our attention has been inward, not global, through most of these 300 years. A "world" sense has come to the United States only since the end of World War II. Regrettably, most of us are still incredibly unfamiliar, uninformed, and naïve in regard to other lands.

DOING YOUR OWN THING

Because our people have come from so many nationalities, there is a far wider range of what is "acceptable" than in some countries where the inhabitants have grown up with a common heritage. As a result, no one needs to feel awkward or uncomfortable in following his own courtesies. Although Americans are noticeably informal, if you prefer somewhat greater formality, feel free to act in your own way. This will be acceptable to those around you. As the young say, each person can "do his own thing" and be respected here to a very large extent.

However, it may help to have a little guidance in understanding the normal pattern of customs in the United States. The subject is, of course, too broad to cover fully, but the following are a few common situations you may encounter.

PERSONAL QUESTIONS

Conversational questions may seem to you both too personal and too numerous—especially when you first arrive.

"Where do you work?" "How many children do you have?" "Do you play golf? What is your score?" "Have you taken your vacation yet?" are not personal questions by American standards. They are a search for common ground on which to build a relationship or base a conversation. Understand that such questions are meant to be friendly; the questioner is interested in you; he is not prying or being impertinent, or at least not deliberately so.

This is the way in which we ourselves become acquainted with one another. Since many of us move around the country so often and meet so many people in the course of a year, we tend to "telescope" these exploratory courtesies. We meet, and by rapid questioning we establish what we feel to be an easy understanding, for we know that in this fluid country we may soon lose this person in the normal ebb and flow of life.

In less mobile countries people operate from a different basis. They erect defenses of a social nature to protect their privacy and their position; they hold off any moves toward intimacy until there has been adequate time to assess the newcomer and weigh him in the balance. Only then do they feel comfortable in discussing anything as personal as their children, or where they live, or what they do at work. The difference is more of timing than of intent. Americans move faster, living like a movie that is run at double speed, because tomorrow they may have been transferred across the country or you may be back across the sea. "If we flow apart again, we will at least have had today," say the Americans.

To those coming from countries where opening amenities are normally handled more slowly, over a longer period of time, the American way can seem like an abrupt barrage of questioning, almost frightening in its personal intensity. Even here there are subjects which are avoided, being considered too personal and therefore impolite even by our relaxed standards! These include questions about a person's: a) age; b) financial affairs; c) cost of clothes or personal belongings; d) religion; e) love (or sex) life.

If you are asked these or any other questions which seem to you to be too personal, you need not answer them. You can simply smile or say pleasantly that you "do not know" or "In my country that would be a funny question," or turn the questions gently aside by some comment such as "Isn't it interesting to see how different nationalities begin a conversation?" or some similar deterrent. If you do that, follow it quickly with another topic, or make some comment of your own on variations in customs, or lead the conversation off in some other direction. The American will not be offended, but he will get the point.

INTRODUCTIONS

The whole matter of names is a "culture shock" to many people. Americans have a minimum feeling for "rank," especially socially.

Most do not themselves enjoy being treated with special deference for age or position; it makes them uncomfortable. Many Americans find even the terms "Mr.," "Mrs.," or "Miss" stiff and formal. You hear people well beyond middle age say—even to quite young people—"Just call me Sally (or Henry or Don)." Being on first-name terms is taken as a sign of acceptance and friendliness. However, this need not bother you. If you are not comfortable in following the boss's immediate request to "Call me Andrew," it is quite all right. Just smile and say "After a while perhaps, but thank you anyway" (meaning, for feeling that friendly!).

Quite normally, introductions are made right from the start with first names: "Mary Smith, this is John Jones." This then leaves the option open to you; you can call the lady "Mary" or you can call her "Miss Smith"—whichever you prefer. Sometimes both of you use last names for a few minutes, then one or the other (or both) lapse into first names. The host has given you the choice. If you don't want to use first names so quickly, just don't. Nobody will mind.

You may notice that when Americans speak together they almost never use each other's names or titles in conversation. We have no equivalent to "Alors, Mademoiselle. . . ." If you are accustomed to hearing such forms of address interspersed throughout a conversation, their lack may feel cold or impersonal at first. Feel perfectly free to drop in your own "Madame," "Señor," "Herr Doktor," or the actual name if you want to do so. It will sound "interesting," different, and a bit flattering to the American! But do not be offended if we do not do it too.

TITLES

Waves of people who have come to settle in the United States have discarded the whole concept of "high and low estate." Status titles are associated with class distinctions—Lord Apley, Count Bernard, the Marchioness of Something. . . . Since class differences are minimized in this country, we do not have family titles, although we comply if visitors carry them. What we do use instead, however, if a person is distinguished, are *occupational* titles. These are considered to be different, denoting a recognition that has been *earned,* not merely inherited. Occupations which most frequently carry titles include: diplomats, members of the Senate (or certain other top government posts), judges of the courts, military officers above a certain rank, medical doctors, ranking professors, priests, rabbis, and some Protestant clergy.

Examples would be: Ambassador Jones, Senator Smith, Governor Rockefeller, Judge Harley, General Clark, Dr. Brown (medical), Dr. Green (Ph.D.), Father White, Rabbi Cohen, Dr. (or Bishop) Gray.

Generally speaking, men in all other occupations are addressed as "Mister." If in doubt as to the manner of address, never hesitate to ask. If you are embarrassed to ask, yet want to be respectful, you can always use "Sir." The man you address will probably realize your dilemma and help you by telling you the proper term.

But unless you are distinguished, you will find all formalities in address are quickly lost. You will not hear Herr Studienrat or Direttore or Señora for long because a friendly, informal relationship is more important to Americans than is either rank or status. We can still respect a person deeply even if we call him Charlie or Pedro. To us, respect and informality are not related.

DEFERENCE

There are other lacks in addition to titles that visitors accustomed to chauffeurs, servants, and considerable attention at home may find insulting at first. A man may consider that insufficient deference has been paid in relation to his position when he is treated like everyone else here. Since the United States is a "do-it-yourself" country, we generally carry our own bags, take our laundry to the laundromat, stand in line at the grocery store, or shine our own shoes, whoever we may be—lawyer, professor, bank president, or corporate executive. Service in the States is purely a matter of cold cash; it has nothing to do with deference, respect, position, race, nationality, or personality. Whoever can afford the extremely high cost of service in this country and wants to buy it, may. But there is absolutely no social stigma in doing one's own daily chores, no matter how menial. In fact, many Americans who could afford household help or a driver or a gardener do not employ them. They prefer family privacy, independence, freedom from responsibility, all of which are at least partially lost when one has help in one's home. Others would rather use their money for travel, sport, or in some other way instead of paying high American wages for domestic help.

PROTOCOL

Similarly, those coming from countries where rank is clearly shown feel the lack of protocol. We do not bow more deeply, or a greater number of times, to some people than to others to show respect; we rarely seat an honored guest in a particular position in a living room or in a car. The few formalities you may observe are that the "honored guest" will normally sit to the right of the host or hostess at a dinner party and he will probably be shown through a door or into an elevator first. However, if this presents any delay or blocks the passageway, the nearest person (rather than the most honored) may often go through first without implying any disrespect at all.

In Japan the back seat is the honored place in a car. If we have any feeling for this at all, it is likely that the front seat, next to the driver, is considered the best in a private car, partly because the driver is likely to be the host himself and partly because the front window offers the best view.

BLUNT SPEECH

Because we Americans come from varied backgrounds, many of us lack full social graces and have remarkably small vocabularies. Don't think we are being rude if we tend to speak in monosyllables or answer with a mere "O.K.," "Sure," or "Nope," or greet you with "Hi." Our brevity is not a personal insult, though to those accustomed to gracious phrases we are (and will seem) blunt. How much more courteous it is to use the Japanese phrase "Osore irimashita"—"I am overpowered with admiration"—in a shop, for example, than just to say "Too expensive" and turn away. Both make it clear that since the price is too high the speaker is not going to buy, but the Japanese way is undoubtedly more gracious!

WE ARE EASILY EMBARRASSED

Americans are sometimes blunt from embarrassment too. They often find it awkward to respond gracefully if people compliment them or thank them at any length. They are likely to brush aside such courtesies and "turn people off" from embarrassment; not as experienced or poised as one would think, they simply do not know what to say! Their intent is not to be rude; in fact they really like your courtesy but cannot express a graceful response. Except for Christmastime, there is not a great deal of gift-giving in the United States, so you will find Americans may be embarrassed as they accept gifts, especially if, being unprepared, they have nothing to give you in return. We are, on the whole, a warm but unpolished people!

SILENCE

Many Americans find silence uncomfortable. They will babble on to fill any quietness if it extends for more than a moment. Students often study with their radios blaring; housewives leave televisions on for the "companionship" of sound even though they may be working in some other room. If you are silent for long periods, they will do their best to "draw you out" or will ask if you feel all right or if there is anything they can do to help you. One aspect of silence can be confusing however: if Americans disagree with what you are saying, many of them will remain quiet. This may not indicate agreement; often it only means that they consider it impolite to argue further.

PRIVACY

Often perplexing to those newly arrived from other lands is our lack of desire for privacy. We are not a nation of hedges and walls, of gates and inner courts. Our lawns run into one another without fences; we leave our office doors open while we work; we run in and out of each other's houses without telephoning first, often without even ringing the doorbell.

This is a big country. Its inhabitants have never lived in walled cities or had to protect themselves from warring princes in neighboring states. During our first centuries, America was so sparsely populated that neighbors were something to be longed for—they were not fenced out. A new face or new arrival was a cause for rejoicing. In the covered-wagon days when this nation was first being developed, people lived cooperatively or not at all. They turned their wagons inward and came together in the circle of firelight for safety. They protected one another in teams, they shared their sweat and labor jointly as together they cut down forests, laid railroads, roofed barns, or husked fields of corn. They deeply depended on each other in all phases of life.

Out of these early days has come a heritage of openness rather than privacy. It shows itself in many little ways; you will feel it as you visit in our houses: rooms without doors or with half walls, no walls, or glass walls. In reverse we feel the opposite when we travel;

we are surprised to find doors constantly shut throughout homes and offices. Part of the answer may lie in central heating. The thing to remember is this: lack of concern for privacy is a difference of custom to be understood but not to be fretted over. If colleagues wander into your office without knocking, or if people forget to close your door when they leave the room, don't be upset. Help them to learn that you would like it to be otherwise, or else adjust yourself to new ways. But in either case, be patient with the difference. It goes a good deal deeper into our roots than even most of us realize. Most Americans actively *dislike* the feeling of being enclosed in a room. They prefer an open doorway; unconsciously they miss a sense of space, a feeling of "breathing room," the sounds and flow of everyday life. They feel, as they say, "boxed in" when they find themselves in a tightly shut room. "Don't Fence Me In" could be our national song!

DISTANCE AND BODILY CONTACT

Did you know that all human beings have a "comfort zone" regarding the distance they stand from someone when they talk? This distance varies in interesting ways among people of different cultures.

Greeks, others of the Eastern Mediterranean, and many of those from South America normally stand quite close together, often moving their faces even closer as they warm up in a conversation. North Americans find this awkward and often back away a few inches; studies have found that they tend to feel most comfortable at about 21 inches apart. In much of Asia and Africa, there is even more space between two people in conversation. This greater space subtly lends an air of dignity and respect, an amplitude of time. This matter of space is nearly always unconscious, but it is interesting to observe.

This difference applies also to the closeness with which people sit together, the extent to which they lean over one another in conversation, how they move as they argue or make an emphatic point. In the United States, for example, people try to keep their bodies apart even in a crowded elevator; in Paris they take it as it comes!

Although North Americans have a relatively wide "comfort zone" for talking, they communicate a great deal with their hands —not only with gestures but also with touch. They put a sympathetic hand on a person's shoulder to demonstrate warmth of feeling or an arm around him in sympathy; they nudge a man in the ribs to emphasize a funny story; they pat an arm in reassurance or stroke a child's head in affection; they readily take someone's arm to help him across a street or direct him along an unfamiliar route. To many people—especially those from Asia or the Moslem countries—such bodily contact is unwelcome, especially if inadvertently done with the left hand. Many Americans are left-handed; there is no awareness at all here of any social significance of left or right. In all such matters, however, if it disturbs you, a slight hesitation on your part will usually be felt and heeded.

In much of the world, handholding and kissing in public have become commonplace. Certainly it is true in the States. One merely ignores what one sees and passes on.

Chapter 3

Some American Ideas
Are Different: Personal

CRITICIZING AUTHORITY

In much of the world, authority is not challenged either out of respect or out of fear; sometimes, too, because a hierarchy of rank has been fixed for so long that people have been trained for generations never to challenge it.

In such countries children are not expected to question their teachers in school; brilliant young scholars or inventive industrial geniuses are hampered in technical research because young men hesitate to disagree with their "superiors." Clever researchers may be considered too young to have "any right" to present findings that contradict the stereotypes of older men.

The American is trained from childhood to question, analyze, search. "Go look it up for yourself" a child will be told. School tasks are designed to stimulate the use of a wide range of materials. An assignment to "Write a paper on the world's supply of sugar (or the gold standard, or Henry VIII, or Peruvian art)" will send even a young child in search of completely unfamiliar ideas. Even in the primary grades, children are taught to use libraries. By the time they are 14, 15, and 16, many young scholars are making original and valuable contributions in all fields of science from astrophysics to oceanography. Industry is so aware of this untapped resource that each year, through national competitions, it offers tremendous awards among teen-agers in order to seek out (and later employ) the brilliant, inquiring minds which they find scattered across the country.

As seen by members of other nations, this emphasis on questioning and searching is bad for young people's "manners." Foreigners often feel great "lack of respect" in our youth. It is true that many do become cocky and rude and pressing. Foreign visitors are often startled and frequently annoyed to find junior staff members "daring" to challenge older executives or argue points with them; they do not always like it when these young men make detailed but often revolutionary suggestions. One's own blueprints, reports, or analyses may be scrutinized in detail—perhaps even challenged— by a young man. This is not to be considered an insult or loss of face; nor is it an indication of "no confidence." Our whole approach to research is different. We have no personal overtones. Your *ideas* are being looked at, not you yourself. To us the two are quite separate. This is the way our minds work. We are seeking facts; we are not challenging you as a person. So, too, even in social conversations you will find that people often argue, pick an idea apart, ask for your sources or challenge your conclusions. They do not mean to be rude; they are keenly interested and merely trying to explore the *idea* in greater depth.

CONTROLLING NATURE

Many in the world—most Asians, for example—seek to "discover Man's place in Nature." Americans try instead to "control" nature. We speak of "harnessing" a river; "conquering" space; "taming" the wilderness. Asians (and many others) think more in terms of "compromise," "consensus," or "harmony." Americans believe anything can be done "if we just put our minds to it." They say: "The difficult can be done today; the impossible takes a little longer." So the searching, challenging—often arrogant—mind goes to work. Nothing is left to Allah, to Fate, or to Time to solve.

Fortunately, we are beginning to realize that Man cannot "control" Nature. We are coming to understand how we have wasted and spoiled and polluted for the sake of transient gain. We are worried now about the nation's resources, the ugliness, the "urban sprawl." You will read about this in our newspapers and hear it discussed widely wherever you go.

Possibly a similar note of withdrawal is taking root in our international posture as well!

ORDER AND INITIATIVE

In many nations the very fabric of life depends on planning and order; complex formal relationships are preordained by custom. People coming from such traditional countries often consider American ideals of personal initiative or freedom (including the freedom to disagree) and our whole economic system of free enterprise to be chaotic, uncontrolled, and confusing. Some even see them as leading to "anarchy." To them such freedoms are too "loose," too "unstructured" to be comfortable.

At every level this country is working through enormous changes, therefore life in America today does feel "chaotic." The very fiber of the nation is being ripped apart and rewoven; deeplying social attitudes are undergoing tremendous questioning. Is there any *real* morality? Why has the nation never given black people full opportunity? What school subjects are relevant and needed in this fast-paced and technological world? Is marriage outmoded? What is the role of women in today's society?

As you live and work here, you will realize that thousands of Americans are beginning to turn away from the cities in disgust, seeking rural values and quieter lives; much of the old "establishment" is being cast aside; political patterns are shifting; labor-management relationships are being reworked; highly advanced skills that recently were in demand are suddenly no longer needed. The nation is in almost total flux on every front.

This is not necessarily bad for any country. Profound searchings and basic shifts may be useful and necessary. If we handle them well, the nation may come out of them wiser, more moderate, stronger. The only thing certain at this time is that the whole country is in the process of much violent ferment, questioning, and change. These are, therefore, interesting, lively, stimulating, but also confusing times in American history. Those who come to the country during this transitional period must try hard to understand, rather than pass judgment too quickly on the confusion that they will certainly feel and see.

TRUTH OR COURTESY?

Just as our degree of individual freedom seems "loose" and therefore uncomfortable to many foreign visitors, foreign attitudes toward truth often seem "loose" and uncertain to Americans.

In many countries people will tell you what they think you want to hear, whether or not it is true. To them, this implies politeness. To Americans, it is considered misleading—even dishonest—to distort facts on purpose, however kind the motive. The point is—our priorities are different; in the United States truth has a higher priority than politeness. We are taught from babyhood that "Honesty is the best policy." Elsewhere, courtesy, a man's honor, family loyalty, male machismo, or many other values might come far ahead of honesty if one were listing priorities. But with us, trust and truth are of paramount importance. If we say of a man, "You cannot trust him," this is one of the most damning statements that can be made about him.

In view of such profound differences about values, it is natural that misunderstandings and irritations often occur, especially in exact areas such as the negotiation of contracts. A Mexican has said, "With us a business deal is like a courtship." Americans lack this grace, but on the other hand you can count on their word. You know where you are with them; except in advertising, they will not be "whispering sweet nothings" that they do not mean in order to make you feel desirable!

"How far is it to the next village?" the American asks a man standing by the edge of the road. In some countries, because the man realizes that the traveler is tired and eager to reach his destination, he will politely say "Just down the road." He thinks this is more encouraging, gentler, and therefore the wanted answer. So the American drives on through the night, getting more and more angry, feeling "tricked." He thinks the man deliberately lied to him, for obviously he must have known the distance quite well.

Had conditions been reversed, the American would feel that he was "cheating" the driver if he implied the next town was close when he knew it was really 15 miles further on. Although he, too, would be sympathetic to the weary driver, he would say "You have a good way to go yet; it is at least 15 more miles." The driver might be disappointed, but he would at least know what to expect.

This oft-repeated question of accuracy versus courtesy leads to many misunderstandings between people of different cultures. If you are aware of the situation in advance, it is sometimes easier to recognize the problem.

PERSONAL PROGRESS AND JOB-HOPPING

In many parts of the world, "personal influence" is almost essential in getting ahead. One needs a "godfather," a "sponsor." Here that is not true. Naturally all people use "influence" sometimes, but one rarely advances far on that basis alone in the United States. Here means of success are generally considered to be: the willingness to work hard (at any kind of job), scholarship or skill, initiative, an agreeable and outgoing personality. In other words, even in the realm of personal progress, this is a "do-it-yourself" society. By and large, success is neither inherited nor bestowed. This means, therefore, that our employment practices are different from those in many other countries.

In some nations it is considered disloyal to quit a job; deep reciprocal loyalties exist between employee and employer (recipient and "patron" in many cases); lifelong job security and family honor are frequently involved.

This is not true in the United States. "Job-hopping" is part of our constant mobility. We consider it a "right" to be able to better ourselves, to move upward, to jump from company to company if we can keep qualifying for more responsible (and therefore better) jobs.

This interchangeability of personnel seems unreasonable to some members of foreign nations. Where are our roots? How can we be so cold and inhuman? "We act," some say, "as if we were dealing with machines, not humans." They do not understand that a great many Americans *like* to move about. New jobs present new challenges, new opportunities, new friends, new experiences—often a new part of the country.

The employer may be quite content too. Perhaps he has had the best of that man's thinking; a new person may bring in fresh ideas, improved skills, or new abilities. Then, too, a newcomer will probably start at a lower salary for he will have no seniority. "Hopping" is so readily accepted here, in fact, that a good man may "bounce" back and forth among two or three corporations, being welcomed back to his original company more than once through his career, each time at a different level.

WEALTH, PRIVILEGE, AND THE MASS MARKET

Status symbols such as cars, color television sets, and swimming pools often confuse visitors to the States. Most Arabs, Latins, and Africans, for example, are accustomed to a two-class system in which privilege exists only when accompanied by wealth. Classes are polarized and there are just two: rich and poor. A luxury market supplies a small number of expensive goods for the rich; everyone else does without.

In the United States this is not true. Because in our economy we operate on the basis of a mass market, blue-collar workers, miners, farmers, even people on welfare own goods that represent great wealth elsewhere. In terms of hours-of-work, the cost for such luxuries here is low. Understandably the man from Ecuador, for example, assumes that the owner of a car in the United States is as rich as an Ecuadorian car owner has to be. Actually he is not; stenographers, high school students, or janitors can and do buy cars, trips abroad, all kinds of luxuries on the installment plan—as do most other people. The costs over a reasonable period of time are not prohibitive in terms of their wages.

This difference can be perplexing for the visitor who, understandably, interprets wealth in his terms, thinking a Cadillac car and mink coat *must* indicate high class and therefore education. As a result he expects to find that the owner possesses the cultural level that he thinks accompanies leisure. In America this is not necessarily so. Quick money comes from all kinds of sources; "rags to riches" is still a common U.S. occurrence. The opulent money spender is not necessarily either educated or cultured—in fact, he is usually neither!

TRADITIONAL ECONOMY

Elite 3%–5%

Middle class 15%

Farmer, worker, underemployed 80%

MODERN (U.S.) ECONOMY

Elite 5%–10%
Middle class (including most farmers and workers) 70%–75%
Underemployed 10%–15%

(From Bryant Wedge, Director, Institute for the Study of National Behavior —used with permission.)

CLASS

America likes to claim that it is a "classless" society. Maximum wages, a high standard of living, mass-produced clothing, purposefully casual speech, and the wide use of first names all combine to give the nation an affluent, classless appearance, especially to newcomers. But, under this professedly equal "veneer," the United

States is, in fact, markedly segmented into neighborhoods, residential areas, and ghettos; right and wrong sides of town.

The important difference, however, between this country and many others is that in the United States it is easy for people to move from one class to another on their own merits, rather than by birth, and to become an accepted part of a new setting. To do so, a person needs enough energy, determination, and ability to make a real success of *something*. He can start as a salesman, factory hand, riveter, taxi driver, trainee, or bank teller. . . . Americans love—and many are themselves living proof of—the "Self-made Man." You can hear these stories all around you if you ask people about their youth: the man whose father was a miner but he himself is now a leading journalist; the man who put himself through school by selling brushes but now is president of the brush company. . . . These are the dramatic stories, but for everyone who gets right to the top there are thousands of others who, less dramatically but nonetheless truly, move many steps beyond their parents on the social ladder.

This constant flow of people from one social level to another indicates that both the word and the idea of "class" mean something so different in the United States from most other countries that the whole subject needs to be considered here. Not only is this nation made up of highly diverse ethnic, racial, and social strands, as we have noted, but, as we have also said, its inhabitants are enormously mobile geographically. People shift and move across its length and breadth to a remarkable degree. One statistical study reports that one out of five families moves every three years!

This ceaseless mixing and merging in new communities, this repeated adjustment to new environments and new people, is an important factor in trying to understand the baffling question of "class" in America. The "do-it-yourself," independent, questioning American personality is another factor.

In many lands a man's social position is still a group matter, shared with his family, his wider group of relatives or clan, perhaps even his whole village or district. Not so the American's. In the

United States, position in society is, to a large degree, personal rather than family or group.

Before World War II, family feeling was strong in America too. Uncles, aunts, grandparents, and children of all ages vacationed with one another, came together for holiday festivities, and were a closely knit unit. But as technology takes hold in any nation, social patterns are bound to change. The mathematician or scientist suddenly is in great demand and moves faster than his colleagues into new prominence; he rises up out of any social class; technological jobs and new plants require firms to send men to new areas, removing them from stable family ties; more and more people settle in small houses in urban areas where grandparents and other family members can no longer share space.

The same shift is already taking place in most new countries. Nowadays a man who can read and understand the newspaper or fix a tractor may, and often does, take over from the traditional leader or chieftain. Technology puts a premium on youth which better understands electronics, computers, atomic energy, and the space age. Young people move ahead, starting new families in new ways. As people learn complicated modern skills, their wages rise; the "onward and upward" ferment becomes more and more widespread; traditional classes and positions are torn apart by the force of twentieth-century demands.

Frequently it is just one member of a family who surges ahead. He may become president of a university, head of a firm, or a well-known member of government; meanwhile the rest of the family remain in modest jobs in a modest environment. When this happens, many Americans feel no psychological commitment either to their relatives or to their community. Some, of course, maintain strong ties of affection and loyalty, but for many, new frontiers beckon. They may come back now and then to their former environment, but many move away, never to return.

Most nations derive considerable security from basic, stable, lasting human ties. For them each person is embedded in a lifelong and supportive network of family and community relationships.

However, the American, seemingly self-sufficient but rootless, rarely can take his own position for granted. Throughout life, most Americans keep on making new alliances, losing them, moving on to others. For most people "class" is a competitive and changing thing. Class edges, therefore, are blurred.

Studies show that four out of five Americans, when asked, describe themselves as "middle class." In most other countries higher percentages of people tend to define "class" more closely and therefore describe themselves either as "upper class" or "lower class"; many even subdivide "middle" into either "upper or lower middle." Nowadays few Americans think in terms of "lower-middle-upper." Especially among the young, this former system of stereotyping is breaking down. Race, ethnic background, region, city, and religion are all merging in new ways. The words "culture" or "counterculture" are replacing the word "class," and the whole social structure is undergoing profound changes. Much of our so-called "middle class" has been migrating to suburbia and been replaced in the cities by new combinations of ethnic and racial groups.

"Success" can be defined as that which gives a man (or woman) more power than he possessed before. It can be won through skill, brains, leadership, sometimes sheer perseverance, regardless of birth. In the American scene "success" has normally been accompanied by increased financial rewards. The "upward-moving man," therefore, has traditionally found himself associating with first one and then another "success level," with its accompanying money level.

As a result, "class" in the United States has been determined both by a person's job and his pattern of consumption. Since "class" is a flexible, competitive matter, people try to make their position clear by visible and recognizable symbols such as cars, houses, clubs, vacations, and so on. As someone has said, "Middle-class America progresses from the little Cape Cod to the split-level with the dropped living room, and on to the larger house with a panelled den." Those considered "below" are subtly rejected by many, lest association with them drag down those who consider themselves further up the social ladder. Racial and ethnic discrimination should be seen, in this country, against the background of a much broader but less discussed tendency of many Americans to "exclude" one another—of any color—through fear of losing their own place. Much that is thought to be racial prejudice here is in fact as much cultural prejudice. "Poor Whites" in the South, for example, fear the rise of Blacks on an educational and job-threat basis as well as merely for skin color. This feeling of job-threat plays a large part, also, in the widespread union blockage of black membership.

Youth is in the process of developing a different set of goals and criteria. What they call the "Establishment" seems to them to be both empty and false. Mr. John Stone, Episcopal Chaplain at Princeton University,* describes their search as looking for a system that "can stand the test of being more inclusively human." He suggests that the young of today prefer a terrain of peaks and valleys rather than "a plateau of prosaic (but illusory) safety" which they feel has been the goal of recent generations.

Mr. Stone describes some of their judgments as follows: "Suddenly to be white is no big deal . . . to be a policeman or a judge is only being a border guard on middle-class turf." A doctor is "an exploiter of middle-class illness" and a businessman "an exploiter of middle-class greed." College to many of them becomes "a middle-class union card leading into the middle-class managerial net." Service in the army is no longer seen as an honorable duty but as "professional killing."

The attitudes of youth, various shifting status symbols, and many new social trends are complex and difficult even for Americans to interpret; no one will expect you to do so. However, if you can understand that in America social position is not a stable, inherited factor, you will comprehend much about the nation.

Whenever any society is mobile and competitive, tensions are in-

---

* (*On Pilgrimage: Marriage in the 70's* by John H. Snow, Seabury Press, New York, 1971.)

evitable. You will be acutely aware of social tensions in American life. Could it be, however, that stress and strain are needed—any-where—for full national vitality?

In order to fulfill its function, a watch or clock must be both under tension and in motion. Might the same be true also of a nation—or a man?

Chapter 4

Some American Ideas
Are Different: National

BLACK AMERICANS

A cherished American myth is that this nation is a great melting pot, a haven for the oppressed.

In fact, as we said earlier, it is not a "melting pot" at all. This is one of the deep reasons underlying the fast-shifting social patterns of today. This country was founded almost wholly by "WASP's"— White, Anglo-Saxon, mostly Protestant people. As one discovers by reading American history books, they have never truly recognized the contributions made by any other incoming groups—Negro, Mexican, Italian, Japanese, Chinese, Irish. . . . Members of these groups have worked hard to become "assimilated," where possible —that is, to take on "WASP" characteristics and become a part of the white American culture. But for those with racial features which could always be recognized, assimilation has not been possible. As the years have passed, the proportion of WASP's to other Americans has radically changed. WASP's are now a marked minority in many parts of the country. The new majorities, having been rejected over the years, understandably are turning back to their own ethnic and racial backgrounds, seeking their own pride and identity out of their own past histories. The largest and most noticeable of these groups is, of course, the 11 percent of the nation who are black.

The whole question of their changing role in American society has been so played up in the world's headlines that visitors to our shores often expect to find police dogs, mob scenes, and bar fights everywhere when they arrive. They are likely to be surprised when instead they see Blacks and Whites working side by side in offices, factories, schools, and institutions in cities across the country. Not everyone realizes that the majority of Negroes are urban, congregated in and around a relatively small number of U.S. cities. Large areas of agricultural America have almost no Negroes at all, sometimes from bigotry but often also from Black choice.

Many dark-skinned people arrive here fearing personal attack or expecting various degrees of apartheid. Slights, insults, and narrow-minded boycotting do still take place unfortunately, especially in the crucial areas of housing, schools, and jobs. There are still frictions and outbursts; school equality is, to our shame, still a dream and not a reality; there are still too many areas of the country where black people do not enjoy the full range of opportunities available to Whites.

However, the overwhelming majority of Americans are finally working, studying, and sharing facilities together, including restaurants, bathing areas, concert halls, parks, and rest rooms. This was not true even a few years ago, so progress is slowly being made. You will be able to observe this as soon as your plane lands. You will see it in the airport, in public buses and trains, in movie houses and eating places, in department stores and libraries, in offices and plants. Real friendships between the races, full trust, easy social encounters are still far too rare. However, even in this—the slowest area of progress—barriers are gradually breaking down, especially among the young.

Because the world press has concentrated mostly on the negative scene with little reference to any kind of progress, newcomers may at first be surprised at the economic range they will find among black Americans. They will see many Blacks who own good cars, fine homes, and stylish clothes. Colleges are opening the way to better jobs; black executives, judges, and professors are no longer rare; more and more Negroes are buying houses and apartments in formerly all-white areas and sending their children to school with their white counterparts. As everyone knows, this varies by locality and progress is slow, but in the past ten years there has been much forward motion. Those coming from abroad will find a wide gamut of acceptance, but much of it will depend on their own educational background and personality. They need not fear violence or personal attack because of race (though unfortunately both black and white people are too often attacked for other reasons in our cities these days). Black visitors who look for slights and insults will find them; those who do not will encounter much good will, acceptance, and friendship, among both Blacks and Whites.

Writes a young Rhodesian boy studying in all-white, rural South Dakota: "Most of the girls here are white. Some do not mind dating Blacks, some do; some don't date because until they came to college they had never seen a Black and they are sort of scared; but I get along well and am happy." This is probably a fair picture of interracial dating across much of this wide land.

TAX EVASION

Naturally nobody enjoys paying taxes wherever they live. However, where governments back massive welfare, housing, or school programs, and build miles of highways, they must have money. Tax evasion in the United States is considered "fraud" and is looked upon as a serious offense. Computers check the tax returns of rich and poor alike; audits from the Internal Revenue Service are widespread. When rich evaders are caught, they are subject to the same penalty rates that apply to the poor. This is not true in all countries—as many readers well know. But here newspapers feature the action as "front-page scandal" when a wealthy, highly placed person or a corporation is found evading the law. Our legal basis is that "private interests are subordinate to public good." Since tax evasion is regarded as affecting the welfare of the entire community and nation, it is looked upon as a major offense—not worth trying!

MAJORITY-MINORITY COOPERATION

The fact that a minority will peacefully accept the outcome of a hotly contested vote and the idea of cooperation among bitter political adversaries are difficult concepts for many visitors to understand. Some people fear what they call the "tyranny" of the majority. "How does a minority ever get heard?" they ask.

Such people may be interested in attending a town meeting in a small American town. Here anyone may listen as citizens argue hotly, fiercely, loud, and long over some local issue. Finally the vote is called and counted. As the visitor watches, he may see speakers who were bitterly opposed shake hands and offer each other a lift home! The loser does not feel dejected. He will begin straightway again to line up new support (often called lobbying) or he will work on the same issue through some other committee. His loss is taken in good grace: "I have got to work harder to build a bigger majority" is the way he is likely to react. Americans start early to learn the system. From first grade onward in school, they campaign, vote, and elect class committees and even "officers" from among their own number. This is part of the reason for the "Fruit Juice Committee," "Goldfish Feeding Committee," Blackboard Cleaning Committee" or similar rather ridiculous-sounding committees found even as early as in kindergarten classes. The process of voting and the idea of "majority-minority" soon become familiar to Americans. They learn to accept defeat and work toward another day—to live, in other words, within our type of governmental structure.

THE RELATIONSHIP BETWEEN STATE AND NATION

Those who come from lands where the State is supreme find personal initiative in politics baffling; "grass-roots democracy" seems to them chaotic; the relationship among our localities, states, and the nation is hard for them to understand.

To an American the word "State" means one of 50 geographic and fairly autonomous units, united by our rather loose Federal Government. But to a Frenchman, a Russian, a Syrian, a Korean, a Congolese, or to many others, the word "State" means a strongly centralized national government with absolute powers far beyond those held by our federal authorities. To those accustomed to any form of "Strong Man (or Strong Committee) rule," be they from South America, Asia, Africa, or elsewhere, a strongly centralized authoritarian power is normal and comfortable. Such people expect a leader to act decisively, quickly, and alone. They do not understand the American preference for compromise, committee decision, or consultation with many "lesser" people, some of whom may, in fact, be the "Strong Man's" enemies. Long delays or legal "quibbling" while our government "tests the winds of public opinion" are often mistakenly interpreted as meaning that our President does not really care about the question or is, in fact, not sincere in his stand.

Visitors often ask: "How can a local legislature defy *national* authority?" How, for example, can there still be segregation in American schools when almost 20 years ago the nation's Supreme Court ruled that it was unconstitutional? Does this mean, they ask:

1) that there is no strength in the "Central" government? (IF so, why do they not call out the army to enforce their ruling and show strength?)

2) that the whole system is a sham—a show of empty words? Is it all hypocrisy?

Because of its enormous size and the great variety of its people, the United States has developed a system that allows for doing things gradually (although, in fact, there have been occasions when troops have been called out to enforce a ruling). In constructing a large building, one allows spaces for the stretching and shrinking of metals. We operate on that same principle. Ideas proceed at different speeds in different areas and at different levels of society; an issue packed with emotion in some area takes longer to be resolved there than elsewhere. So the American system was devised with "spaces." Time must be allowed, winds of opinion must be tested, in order to preserve the diversity of this enormous country, while at the same time giving it a basic framework of unity. It is cumbersome and often slow, but precisely because there is leeway, the country has remained a unit despite its share of searing critical differences through the years. If these differences had been met head-on by absolute governmental decree, the nation would almost surely have been fragmented long ago. Many countries face such possible fragmentation within their own borders today because "leeway," gradualism, public opinion, and other safeguards have not been built into their system.

Since public opinion is so vitally important in America, our leaders *must* work within its boundaries. To do so, they must keep consulting, compromising, conferring, and "feeling the pulse" of the nation. Those who are accustomed to public institutions being the instruments of a Central Government naturally look for a unified "line" somewhere in the United States; they do not find it. They assume a country *reflects* government policy. In fact, in the United States it is more usual for public opinion to *direct* government policy. The American people, for example, demanded withdrawal from Vietnam long before the government took that stand. Black and white citizens marched and struggled and demonstrated together for civil rights so long and hard and steadily that the Supreme Court ruling on desegregation finally resulted; it was not initiated by the government but by the people themselves.

What newcomers need to understand is that we Americans recognize differences and allow leeway among: 1) the law; 2) policy; and 3) the actual situation. These three factors often pull and tug just as a ship creaks and strains when its hull meets conflicting winds and waters. But there are two important points: 1) It remains a ship and 2) It continues to move ahead, however slowly. It does this because it has play in its joints. Therefore it does not founder but can stay afloat even under heavy stress.

Let us look again at the deeply divisive national problem of civil rights:

1) *The Law:*   By federal law there are now neither legal nor constitutional discriminations against Negroes.

2) *Policy:*   The federal policy is: Discrimination is illegal and should be phased out "with all possible speed."

3) *The Facts:* All too slowly, with uneven pace, sometimes two steps forward and one step back, faster in some states than in others, America is gradually moving toward a real equality.

The country is struggling with countless other serious issues that occur at national, state, local, and personal levels. It will undoubtedly continue to struggle with all of them for a long time, gradually working out accommodations and resolving various kinds of problems. Despite all kinds of deep regional, emotional, and personal differences, the nation will be kept on course throughout this process by the law of the land.

It is often difficult for those from highly centralized nations to understand, but the fact is that final power really *does* lie in the hands of the people in the United States. This is true whether one speaks of political, economic, or social power. Americans distrust and will not long tolerate being "pushed" by a Strong Man or a strong government. They want to keep power decentralized; they like it that way. Social changes, therefore (such as civil rights, divorce laws, equality of pay for women, abortion laws), are debated long, hard, and often terribly slowly at state leve. National law reflects many *state* differences and attitudes. Change comes heartbreakingly slowly after endless debate. But those changes which finally become the law of the land do so eventually with the work, the thought, and the consent of a nationwide majority. Most laws, therefore, remain stable once achieved.

AMERICANS THINK FROM SMALL TO LARGE

Americans tend to move from the specific and small to the general and large; we have just seen an example of this in the fact that they progress from personal and local issues to the state and finally to the nation—not the other way around.

Many other people, including Italians, Russians, Japanese, and most South Americans, tend to move the other way: it is more comfortable for them to start with a general or universal idea and then narrow it down to specific facts. The difference between these two approaches is subtle and usually unrecognized in daily life. Actually, however, it lies at the root of many everyday misunderstandings and irritations among peoples of different cultures.

Let us take as simple an example as the addressing of envelopes. Many who start with the general and move to the particular begin the address with the country; then they write the prefecture (or province, department, county, or state); then the city; the district of the city; the street; and finally the number of the actual house. In the United States people start with the smallest item, namely the number of the house. The address then moves on to the larger divisions: the street, the town, the state, and finally the country.

This totally opposite approach to thinking affects many negotiations, plans, or attitudes, whether we recognize it or not. If an Indian, Japanese, or Mexican asks an American about an overall goal, a basic theory, or a principle, he often feels buried under detail in the answer he gets. He is confused by a flood of statistics or a long description of *method* before he hears any overall purpose or plan. People say: "Ask an American the time and he tells you how to build the clock!" Americans, on the other hand, feel equally frustrated when they ask for a specific fact or detail but then are subjected to 20 minutes of theory, philosophy, or universality without a single concrete fact!

Neither of us can—or will want to—change our lifetime patterns of thought. However, it may help us both if we recognize the possibilities of difference along these lines.

Chapter 5

Manners and Courtesies in Social Life

FRIENDSHIPS

In this mobile country of ours, friendships can be close, constant, intense, generous, and real, yet fade away in a short time if circumstances shift. Neither side feels hurt by this. Both may exchange Christmas greetings for a year or two, perhaps a few letters for a while—then no more. If the same two people meet again by chance, even years later, they pick up the friendship where it left off and are delighted. This can be perplexing to those from countries where friendships flower more slowly but then become lifelong attachments, with mutual obligations, extending sometimes deeply into both families.

In the United States you can feel free to visit in people's homes, share their holidays, enjoy their children and their lives without fear that you are taking on a lasting obligation. Do not hesitate to accept hospitality because you cannot reciprocate. No one will expect you to do so for they know you are far from home. Americans will enjoy welcoming you and be pleased if you accept their friendship easily.

Another perplexity for many people from other countries is that, although Americans include them warmly in their personal everyday lives, they do not demonstrate a high degree of courtesy if it requires a great deal of time. This is the opposite of the practice in some nations where people are unstintingly generous with their time, but do not necessarily admit a guest into the privacy of their home. In some places hosts will appear at airports in the middle of the night to meet even a casual acquaintance; they put their car at the visitor's disposal; they take days off to act as a guide—all evidence of tremendous generosity. But these same people may never introduce their wives or invite the guest to participate in their family life. In both cases the feeling is equally warm; the pattern of expression, however, is different.

Distances, the pace and pressures of life being what they are in America, together with the fact that without household help, cooking, baby-sitting, and other domestic responsibilities must be absorbed into each person's day (as well as all professional, community and social demands), Americans extend their welcome warmly at home but truly cannot manage the time to do a great deal with a visitor outside their daily routine. They will probably expect you to get yourself from the airport to your hotel by public transport; they assume that you will phone them from there; unless you are chairman of the board or a similar dignitary you will probably be expected to find your own way (by cab) from the hotel to the host's office (or home).

However, once you arrive there, the welcome will be full and warm and real. Most visitors find themselves readily invited into many homes here. In some countries it is considered inhospitable to entertain at home, offering what is felt as "merely" home-cooked food, not "doing something" for your guest. It is felt that restaurant entertaining shows more respect and welcome. Or for various other reasons, such as crowded space, language difficulties, or family custom, outsiders are not invited into homes.

In the United States both methods are used, but here it is often considered more friendly to invite a person to one's home than to take him to a public place, except in purely business relationships. The further one is from big cities, the more likely this becomes. So, if your host brings you home with him, do not feel that you are being shown "inferior" treatment.

Don't feel neglected if you do not find flowers awaiting you in your hotel room either. This happens graciously in Thailand, the Philippines, the Caribbean, Holland, and many flower-filled lands. But flowers are exceedingly expensive here, hotel delivery is uncertain, arrival times are often delayed, changed, or canceled—so flowers are not customarily sent as a welcoming touch. Please do not feel unwanted! Outward signs vary in different lands; the inward welcome is what matters, and this will be real.

PARTIES

Among the more interesting things to observe as you travel the world are the varied ways in which people conduct themselves at parties. In some countries men and women drift to opposite ends of the room and talk to one another; in others they sit in large chairs around the edge of the room and talk only to the people on either side of them, or silently eat and observe the scene.

It is normal in some lands for a person to remain patiently silent until he has been introduced, then to talk only to those whom he has "met properly."

As you would imagine, Americans move about a great deal at parties. At small gatherings they may sit down, but as soon as there are more people than chairs in a room—or better yet, a little before this point—you will see first one and then another make some excuse to get to his feet (to fetch a drink or greet a friend or open a window) until soon everyone is standing, moving around, chatting with one group and then another. Sitting becomes static beyond a certain point. We expect people to move about and be "self-starters." It is quite normal for Americans to introduce themselves; they will drift around a room stopping to talk wherever they like, introducing themselves and their wives. If this happens, you are expected to reply by giving your name and your wife's name; then at least the two men generally shake hands. Sometimes the women do so as well, but often they merely nod and smile. A man usually shakes a woman's hand only if she extends it. Otherwise he too just nods and greets her.

After such an informal introduction, you talk together for a little while (here come those questions): "Are you new here?" "How long have you been in America?" "Did you bring your children with you?" Within a moment or two, you will have struck some common ground, conversation will move along for a while, and then *either* couple can feel free to say something informal like: "Well, it's been nice to meet you" or "I hope we see you again soon." This is the signal for both couples to say their "adieus" and drift off to another group.

The basic rule at big parties is: *don't stay in one place for too long.* Pick out people you think look interesting, then go talk to them. Women should not cluster in a group with each other or hide themselves away in a corner. They too move around the room either with their husbands or alone, whichever they prefer, unless they are strategically located (and attractive!) so that people keep coming up to them. The point of a party in this country is to meet and talk with people; the fact that you are all there together under your host's roof is in itself a form of introduction in our view; as a result, anyone can feel free to talk to anyone else.

When you first arrive at a large party, the host or hostess may introduce you to two or three people nearby, but if others are still arriving, he or she may then return to greet newcomers, expecting you to go on by yourself, moving from group to group. If this feels too uncomfortable and frightening, it is quite all right to say to someone: "I am a stranger here and know no one. Could you introduce me to some of the people?" Almost anyone will feel flattered that you turned to him for help and will gladly take you under his wing, introducing you and easing your discomfort.

Our "easy-come-and-go" pattern is unfamiliar to people from most other countries. Like much else about the nation, it stems in large measure from our size, our numbers, and our constantly shifting population.

INVITATIONS

Written

One should answer any written invitation as soon as possible. Some will have R.S.V.P. or "please reply" written at the bottom;

such invitations *require* an answer, but even if such a request is not included, it is still a courtesy to a host to let him know whether (or not) you expect to attend. If a telephone number is given, you can phone; otherwise it is best to write a small note, either accepting or regretting.

By Telephone

When accepting an invitation over the telephone, make it a habit always to repeat four things: 1) the day of the week, 2) the date, 3) the time, and 4) the place. Then you are *sure* you have understood it correctly. If you do not know how to get to the host's home, this is the moment to ask for directions and to *write them down.*

Since telephones are so widespread that communication is easy in the United States, it is considered thoughtless and rude to accept an invitation and then not appear without phoning your regrets *in advance.* If something prevents you from attending, you *always* telephone your host or hostess immediately, just as soon as you know you will not be able to go. Explain the circumstances and express your apologies. Do it *before* the party, as far ahead of time as you can. The host may want to invite someone else in your place or, if you are the guest of honor, may change the date of the party to suit your schedule.

Impersonal

Much social life in this country takes place at communal parties of one kind or another—group activities sponsored by a church, a school, a company division, or a club. These may be dinners, picnics, tours, weekend camping or skiing trips, lectures, concerts, receptions, bowling evenings, or any of a wide variety of affairs. If you have some connection with the sponsoring group, you can assume that you will be welcome to join in any such gathering. Many others are open to you whether or not you have a connection. If you see a poster announcing an event, or read a notice, or find a note in the newspaper, don't wait to be invited. Just go if you can, knowing that no one else will receive a personal invitation either. Such community affairs are friendly and an excellent way to meet new neighbors. If in doubt as to whether or not you would be welcome, just ask someone. But do not feel hesitant just because you were not specifically invited. If it is a cooperative party, do your share of the work and cooperate in the fun too!

WHEN TO ARRIVE AND LEAVE

For meals:

You should arrive at the time you were invited for or within five to seven minutes of that time. If you are very early, walk around the block or wait in your car or downstairs in the lobby. In this country the hostess is also likely to be the cook. Give her those precious last moments in peace to compose her soul; don't arrive *before* the time you were asked for. If you find you are going to be late, it is a real help to your hostess if you telephone and tell her so. She may turn off the stove and be grateful to you for not having spoiled supper by your lateness.

Cocktail parties, receptions, teas:

Invitations for such events usually say "from X hour to Y hour" —5:00 to 7:00 P.M., for example. This means that you can come any time that suits you between those hours. You do not have to leave on the dot of the time indicated, but should go within a half hour at the latest.

For a dance:

It is usual to arrive half an hour to an hour after it starts. There is nothing more dreary than a dance that has not yet gotten under way, unless you are a true dancer who likes the floor uncrowded and the orchestra fresh!

For the theater:

Plan to arrive at least ten minutes before curtain time. You will want to take off your coat, read the program, and settle down before the play begins.

Weddings, funerals, public lectures, sports events:

Be there about ten minutes *before* the specified time so that you will be seated and relaxed by the time it starts.

Business appointments:

Arrive exactly at the moment of appointment or a few minutes *ahead.* It is considered a discourtesy to keep a busy person waiting. If he keeps you waiting, however, take it in good grace. The person whose office is the scene of the meeting takes precedence. If you do not want to give him this advantage, arrange to meet in your office or on some "neutral" ground such as at a club or in a hotel lobby.

DRINKING

Drinking habits vary widely among Americans. Some families never serve any alcoholic beverages. Others have cocktails before dinner, wine with the meal, and/or after-dinner drinks. You are more likely to be offered a cocktail before dinner than to be served wine with the meal. If you are not accustomed to American cocktails, be cautious; they are often quite strong. Ladies as well as men drink them, but you should not feel any hesitation in asking for a sherry, Dubonnet, or nonalcoholic drink (such as Coca-Cola or fruit juice) if you do not want a cocktail. In some homes the cocktail hour may become quite lengthy. If it does and you do not wish to drink additional cocktails, it is perfectly all right to refuse. You can also drink as slowly as you like. It is a good idea to eat some of the food which is offered with drinks; there are usually cheese and crackers, olives, peanuts, potato chips with creamy "dips," or other small offerings.

If the host asks: "What will you have to drink?" you can reply:

"What are the possibilities?" or you may request a particular drink as you prefer.

Common cocktails offered in most homes include:

Gin and tonic:

A particularly popular summer drink made with gin, quinine water, and ice—often with a sprig of mint and slice of lemon or lime.

Scotch or bourbon:

Either type of whiskey is served with water or with soda or "on the rocks." This last phrase means simply that liquor is poured over ice with nothing added. You can ask for "on the rocks with a little water" if you want it somewhat less strong.

Martini:

Colorless but powerful; a short drink made with dry vermouth and gin.

Manhattan:

Sweet and dark colored, made with sweet vermouth and whiskey.

Bloody Mary:

A mild drink, often offered before lunch, made of spiced tomato juice with a "shot" of vodka or gin.

You can have your drinks "straight up" (without ice) or with ice. Iced drinks are not quite so strong, especially after the ice has melted a bit. Americans use more ice than many other nationalities. They also have their drinks "short" or "tall," meaning with or without soda (or water) to fill a tall glass.

When men stop for a drink together on their way home, the one who made the suggestion often pays for the first drink; the companion frequently offers to pay for a second. This is no hard-and-fast rule—they may each pay for their own. Normally if no one extended an invitation but a group of men just find themselves at a bar together, each pays his own bill. Many businessmen have a drink over a business lunch. If you do not want to do this, have no hesitation about declining; it is not a "must." Beer is also often taken at lunch.

Wine is being drunk increasingly in the United States, but it still is not found as commonly as in many other countries. Do not be surprised if you are offered milk, coffee, tea (iced or hot depending on the season), or even Coca-Cola with a meal. Water is not always served, but feel free to ask for it if you want it, either in a home or a restaurant.

WHEN INVITED BY A FAMILY

This is likely to be informal and relaxed. You will probably be served "family style." Platters will be passed from person to person or the host (or hostess) may serve from one end of the table. All ages eat together. The wife who, in this servantless country, has usually prepared the meal often does not wait on table as is customary in many countries. A common family division of labor is for the wife to prepare the meal, the husband to handle the cocktail hour, and the young people or husband, rather than the wife, to change the plates between courses.

Whether or not you help with the dishes afterward will vary depending on your "rank" and age, how often you have been to the home, and family custom. Many families do not permit guests to do any work on the first visit, but if they become frequent guests in the house, then they gradually join in with the various household chores as these occur. Some people *never* let a guest help; it is a good idea to offer, but then take your cue from the response.

Men do a good deal more around the house than is true in other parts of the world. The division of labor varies from household to household, but men frequently take out the trash and help wash the dishes; women normally do the marketing, cooking, cleaning, and laundry. In most households everyone makes his or her own bed except on "clean linen" day; men usually cut the grass and take care of major outdoor jobs; women look after the flower gardens and do much "ferrying" in the family car, especially if there are a number of children, all needing to be taken and fetched from school, sports, dentists, birthday parties, and the like.

At meals it is the custom to wait for the hostess to begin eating and to finish as closely as you can to when everyone else does. Watch your hostess from time to time to judge your own speed. Americans tend to eat rather more quickly than many other people; you may be embarrassed if you find yourself far behind everyone else at the end of the meal.

If for religious (or other) reasons there are some foods you cannot eat, just leave them quietly without calling attention to the fact if possible; otherwise explain in advance to your hostess. Even though at first American food may be different and you may not enjoy it, it will please your hostess if you eat at least some of every dish and express appreciation for her efforts. She will probably have extended herself in trying to please you.

The American habit of shifting the fork from right to left hand when the knife is used—then back again—is unfamiliar to many. Don't feel you must struggle with that system. Either method is perfectly acceptable, so do whatever is comfortable for you. It is *not* considered correct to soak up gravy with bread, to tuck your napkin under your chin, or to make any kind of slurping, burping, or other noises while eating or at the table.

BUFFET MEALS

Buffet meals—called "fork suppers" in England—are a popular means of entertaining because they are informal and easy to handle even without household help. There are no exact rules about what is proper; your hostess will indicate how she wants people to proceed and where they are to sit. You can probably tell just by watching other guests. Systems vary from household to household depending on the way the house is arranged, whether the garden is being used, how many people there are, and so on. Often folding snack tables are provided; if you find it difficult to balance your plate or cut your meat, don't hesitate to seek out the corner of a more solid table and pull your chair up to it so that you are comfortable. Nobody will mind. The point is for people to feel at ease and to have a pleasant, relaxed time together.

You will naturally thank a hostess as you leave, but if you want to be considered really polite and pleasant drop her a note within a day or two after the event. This will be greatly appreciated. If you prefer, you can express your thanks by telephone instead; this should be done on the day immediately following the party. Not everyone does this, but it is not difficult and gives a nice warm feeling that lasts a long time with your host family.

BRINGING GIFTS

Although it is always welcome and gracious, it is not necessary in this country, as it is in some others, to bring flowers or a gift when you are invited for lunch or dinner, except on special occasions such as a birthday or Christmas. If you have visited several times before, you may want to bring an occasional small "thank you" token of appreciation, but generally speaking it is a highly optional matter. We go in and out of each other's houses so informally and so often that gifts are by no means expected. If you do bring something, it should be small and simple—a true "gesture" rather than a gift—perhaps a tiny souvenir of your country or a single rose or a small trinket or a jar of honey or something equally modest.

If you are going to be an *overnight* or *weekend* guest, however, it is customary to bring the hostess a small present—often an appropriate book, a box of candy, a bottle of wine, a small bottle of perfume, or some similar gift.

PRECEDENCE OF MEN AND WOMEN

Who goes first and who follows, and the extent to which women are "emancipated" are some of the remaining variables in today's social world. Women in the United States are reasonably accepted in the business world and even more so in society, in educational establishments, and in community endeavors. They take part in sports activities with their husbands and often travel widely with them, even on business trips. However, despite their growing "equality," most of them still expect, receive, and cherish a number of small special courtesies.

Many men still rise when ladies enter the room on a social occasion—rarely in business—although the custom is fading with the younger generation and under the impact of Women's Lib. Nonetheless, most women (of all ages) still appreciate this courtesy when it occurs!

Men usually open doors for ladies, but then in this country they stand back and allow them to go through first—different from Korea, for example, where women traditionally follow. The exception here may sometimes be for a revolving door; since this is heavy, men normally go first to push for the ladies.

Women in the United States walk *ahead* of men into a room or theater or restaurant unless there is business to be done—such as choosing a table, handling tickets, buying a program. Then the man goes ahead to attend to the details. Women precede men into theater rows or church pews—different from Germany, for example.

In a sense American women have the best of both worlds, both independence and special attention. Some American women can be overwhelming to women whose pattern is more retiring. American ebullience, drive, and energy can seem frightening; they are not meant to be. Some women do appear noisy, aggressive, dominating, but you will find many others who are quiet, content, gentle. The only thing to do is to take each one as she is and make no generalizations until you have observed the women here for several months.

UNESCORTED WOMEN

Women who are alone are far more free here than in many parts of the world; one sees unescorted women of any age everywhere. But, unfortunately, this is a time of great turmoil in the United States. Crime is widespread, and certain precautions are necessary. Except perhaps for hijacking, you can feel safe in airplanes, buses, or trains day or night, although many terminals are best avoided after midnight.

It is safe for a woman to drive long distances alone in her own car if she wants to do so. Service station men and hotel or motel clerks will give friendly help; if there is trouble with the car along the way, a single woman will nearly always get rapid help from passersby or highway patrolmen. She can feel free to accept such help gratefully and readily. But if a woman is driving alone in the city, it is wise for her to keep the doors of her car locked and her purse on the floor or out of sight. These two simple habits could prevent someone from jumping quickly into the car at a stop light or grabbing her purse through an open window.

Cities have become less safe after dark, mostly, alas, because an increasing number of people are stealing or doing desperate things in search of money for a "fix"—the price of the day's drug. The drug problem in the United States is acute and growing. Stay on well-populated streets and well-lighted sidewalks; do not walk in parks at night; take taxis after about 9:00 P.M.

It is perfectly all right for a woman to go alone into a restaurant for either lunch or dinner, with two major exceptions: 1) highly sophisticated, expensive restaurants in big cities and 2) fancy night clubs that have floor shows and/or dancing. Single women should also avoid most public bars, though they can go to cocktail lounges in hotels or good restaurants.

Etiquette varies somewhat across the country as to whether or not a lone woman talks to people at neighboring tables or in adjoining seats. Let your own intuition be your guide. It depends on the appearance of your neighbor and your own personality. Broadly speaking, people get friendlier and more casual as you go further and further west; they tend to be more outgoing in small towns than in large cities as is true in most countries. In today's world it is generally advisable for a single woman not to hold a sustained conversation with a single man who has accosted her in any public place in one of the large cities. A few words and a smile are fine, but if a man pursues a conversation he may well be on the search for a "pickup." Avoid letting him see or overhear your address.

Single women are of course frequently asked to cocktail parties, buffet suppers, picnics, or outings of various kinds. There is no reason why they cannot accept and also return such invitations, inviting single men to their apartments for dinner, or a party either alone or in a group. Women do not offer to pay for meals, taxis, and the like if they have been invited out, but do expect to pay their own way if they go out on business meetings, lunches, or appointments. However, if a man offers to pick up such bills, one accepts graciously. He will probably put it on his expense account anyway!

ADULT DATING

Men and women go out together a great deal, especially in the cities of America; they ski together, work together, dine together, either at restaurants or in each other's apartments. This does not mean that they are necessarily interested in having sex together, though it may appear so and, of course, with some men and women it is so.

To an Arab, an African, or a Latin or to many of the other men of the world, the fact that a girl will so readily go off alone with him often seems to imply that she is "his for the asking." This is not true. It is important to realize this from the start. You will scare off many American girls if you rush in too fast; they may seem very friendly yet have no intention whatsoever of having sex with you at the first meeting or, for that matter, at any time ever. Most American girls are not promiscuous. They may indulge in premarital or even extramarital sex, but generally not unless they feel real affection for the man; and most stay with one man at a time for considerable periods. Most are not looking for "an easy make" and do not appreciate the assumption that they are.

If you have a wife at home, be sure to let this fact be known to the girl early in your acquaintance. It will not necessarily make any difference, but the girl wants to know the situation. She will feel tricked and frequently will drop the man immediately if she thinks he has cheated, lied, or otherwise misled her.

Single men dating American girls should keep their hands off and have more than one date with them before making any move to develop the situation into something more intimate. In today's world of free speech, you can ask a girl how she feels about "going further." But your chances will be poor if you move too fast too soon, regardless of how informal things may look here.

A girl will not feel that she "owes" you sex because you have paid for her dinner. She will feel that her company and her acceptance of you have contributed toward a pleasant evening for both, but not that she "owes" you more. You have to "win" anything beyond a casual friendship by being the kind of person she likes and wants. You cannot "buy" this by offering her a meal or material inducements, as though she were a prostitute.

American girls are accustomed to easy companionability and equality. With the current emphasis on Women's Lib, many are especially touchy about their independence. The "bully" approach never did work well here; nowadays it is completely out. Some men feel that women "like to be dominated"; they boast about how they can "handle" women and feel they can "order," "demand," or "compel" and "have women eating out of their hand." Anyone who comes here expecting to find American girls meek, obedient, or submissive is likely to have a hard time. Today sex is a matter of mutual decision and choice.

Paying for Dates

A general rule of thumb is that a girl in business or college will pay her own way during the day. If, however, a man asks her for something special outside normal working hours—for cocktails or dinner or a dance or the movies—the invitation itself means "come as my guest." If a man wants to accompany her but does not want to pay the bill, he asks differently, thereby letting her know in advance. He will say "Are you planning to go to the football game? If so, shall we sit together?" *or* "I was thinking of going to the theater if I can get tickets. Would you be interested? If so, what price range would suit you?"

The growing sense of male-female equality often includes financial equality too, particularly with young people. Girls find it perfectly normal to pay their way especially if, as is often the case, they are earning the same salary as the man.

The whole matter of "dating" is in transition. Young men and women are quite open and candid in talking over who will pay and for what. You, too, can feel quite free to ask your friends what the situation is wherever you are.

Girls from Abroad

Single girls coming to a job in the United States will often have to work a bit at finding ways to meet men. Men in offices are likely to be family men who rush out at five o'clock to catch a commuter train back home to wife and children; office bachelors often turn out to be wary of dating someone they will see every day. They would rather "have their fun" somewhere else, where no one can carry tales or follow them up too closely.

The best way for a single girl to meet men or other girls easily is likely to be through sports activities or some kind of club. Go skiing or join a bowling team; play golf or tennis; take a membership in a swimming club. If you are not athletic, enroll in an evening class that appeals to both sexes—choosing photography, ballroom dancing, judo, or computer programming, for instance, rather than fashion design, or piano, or pottery! Select your hobby with a little thought!

If you are asked for a "date," remember that you can set the pace. In this country the man generally does the inviting and the planning, but he is likely to find out first what will please the girl. You probably will have an opportunity to indicate the kinds of things you enjoy: mountain climbing or listening to music; being with a group or eating alone together by candlelight. In addition to choosing along such lines, it is you who also set the level of friendship. You can keep things platonic if you want to. If the man seems increasingly affectionate and you want it to be otherwise, you can make that clear. The girl has the choice.

Most big cities contain numerous young men and women who come from elsewhere to work and find it hard to meet new people. Many places therefore have developed what are known as "Singles Clubs." These can be free-for-all marriage markets; they should be avoided. They can also, however, be extremely nice clubs, offering excellent sports facilities, good theater parties, cocktail parties, and the like to help newcomers become acquainted. They usually publish a monthly booklet or have a bulletin board describing the range of activities that will take place that month. If interested, you go to whichever parties or events you choose. If you find congenial people of either sex, that is fine. If not, you drift on home and try again on some other occasion. There are always people at the door to introduce you and make it easy for you to meet and mix, even if you are alone.

Start easily if you join such a group. Be a little cool at first. The super-friendly type who rushes to make friends may in fact be the club bore looking for a new audience. Give yourself time to look over the situation before you become too friendly with anyone.

FINDING "FACILITIES"

A newly arrived Scot was asked what had been the most difficult thing for him on his first day in the United States. Without a moment's hesitation, he answered: "Finding a Men's Room."

Some countries have public conveniences plainly visible on the street or small buildings that are clearly marked. The United States does not. Americans find their way to facilities in such public places as:

gasoline stations—usually clean, also free, though one may have to ask the attendant for a key because they are kept locked when not in use;

restaurants, libraries, museums, department stores, airports; bus terminal or railroad station bathrooms are apt to be unpleasant, but can be found; *never* use the rest rooms in subways. Exhibit halls and all places where the public is welcome are provided with facilities.

You can go into any hotel and use the facilities whether or not you are registered there as a guest; you will usually find them somewhere off the main lobby.

Don't be confused by the name on the door. Sometimes it is marked "Men" or "Women" or "Ladies" or "Dames"; often the term is "Rest Rooms." Especially in restaurants, there may be no word used at all but a picture of an old-fashioned girl or a rooster or some other clue may be painted on the door. Women's rooms are often delicately called "Powder Rooms." The European terms "Comfort Station" or "W.C." are rarely used but generally understood.

If you are in need, just ask for "Men's Room" or "Ladies' Room."

You may need a dime to open the door. In a large hotel or restaurant, leave a tip in the small saucer if there is an attendant—10¢ to 15¢ is common; if you have any special service beyond a towel, you can leave 25¢. One does *not* tip in clubs, but a smile and a friendly word are appreciated.

Chapter 6

Life in the Office

Some office procedures may be unfamiliar.

Again, matters of time and pace crop up. Work days officially start at 9:00 A.M. This should really mean 9 o'clock—not ten past or half past nine. You will find people taking much leeway with starting times, but employers notice this even though they do not necessarily reprimand.

Employees in many nations have a philosophy that one works when the "boss" is present, but any time he is not there, if there is nothing specific or pressing to do, one can relax by reading the newspaper, doing one's fingernails, or otherwise "passing the time" in a personal way. In America one is being paid for one's *time*. Employees are expected to find other work if their own desk is clear, to finish anything pending from previous days, or to help someone else with his work—but never to sit idle. The employer expects value for the money he is spending. He "owns" your time while he is paying for it. The phrase "time is money" means exactly that. The "boss" is not asking more of you than he is doing himself; he will quite probably work through the lunch hour and even take work home at night.

Employee's lunch hours should be kept within the allotted time (unless one is officially discussing company business). Long lunch-time absences may be overlooked now and then, but not habitually. Also, although others may start getting ready to leave the office a few minutes early, new employees should be careful not to cut the day short. Work until the day officially ends at five o'clock.

HIRING AND FIRING

Those from lands where family bonds are close are accustomed to family ties being closely meshed with business connections. This rarely happens in America and is generally mistrusted. We call it "nepotism" and fear it as a corrupting influence or the taking of unfair advantage over "outsiders." Nor do we develop a "patron" or "permanent" relationship between employer and employee. In many countries people relax once they have a job, knowing they will almost never be fired (except for a major immorality). Although there are legal protections in America so that employees cannot be unjustly fired without cause, jobs nevertheless are not permanent. Workers must do a good job, produce well, and get along with their colleagues—or they can be "let go" as it is called. This is rarely done without warning, but it is important to be aware of the fact that in the United States one is a member of a business firm and not a "family." It makes a difference.

INFORMALITY

The informality found in many offices here can prove to be a difficult adjustment for those who are accustomed to clearly defined "rank" in offices. The protocol of rank often exists here too, especially in large city banks, law firms, or major corporations. But in many establishments the atmosphere is loose and easy with considerable joking, teasing, and wandering in and out of offices among all levels of employees. This may be perplexing at first for a newcomer who does not realize that, despite the informal use of first names and bantering chatter, people really know very well who is the "boss." He does, in fact, hold authority, though outward signs may not be clearly visible.

STAFF MEETINGS

Staff meetings are a frequent part of most office routines. Those of all ranks are expected to contribute freely to the discussion if they have something worthwhile to add or suggest. They are not expected to make long speeches nor to speak too many times in the course of a meeting. Make your point briefly and clearly, then be quiet unless asked to develop it more fully. But if you have something worth saying, never hesitate because you feel too inexperienced or too new. People will think you *have* no ideas unless you express them.

COFFEE BREAKS

Nearly all offices have coffee wagons that circulate for midmorning and midafternoon coffee "breaks." Although 15 minutes are allotted twice a day for relaxation and chatter, many employees take coffee to their desks and keep on working.

COLLECTIONS

Don't be startled if someone asks you to make a contribution toward a wedding or retirement present for a fellow employee. This is often done. Everyone contributes a small amount so that a gift can be given in the name of the whole office. You never refuse whether or not you know—or like—the particular recipient. The amount per person is always small, and the requests are infrequent. When you leave, you will have some recognition too!

SOCIAL LIFE

This varies tremendously from office to office. Big corporations may have glee clubs, bowling or baseball teams, trips, dance classes, or other employee activities which you can join or not as you like. Small companies usually do not.

In general people go to lunch with each other by invitation when they so desire; higher rank tends to invite lower rank rather than the other way around, but lines are not closely drawn. Except for special occasions, everyone pays for himself or herself regardless of whether or not an invitation was extended.

It is quite acceptable for men or women colleagues, single or married, to go out together to lunch. This may be the extent to which your office "friends" will invite you. Although in general Americans readily take people home with them, they often do not want to mix business and social life. If this is the case in your place of work, you will have to seek your friendships through other channels.

If people rush quickly out of the office in the evening without any courtesies, think nothing of it. Often they must travel long distances to get home and are hurrying to catch special trains or buses.

Chapter 7

Size, Time Zones, Climate, and Clothes

SIZE

It is difficult to really experience or "feel" the size of the United States even when you know the actual number of miles from coast to coast. To get the full impact, one should realize, for example, that it takes 48 hours (two long days and two long nights) to travel by train from Chicago to Los Angeles, rolling along hour after hour across wheat fields, mountains, and deserts. Chicago is a full overnight train trip from New York.

Another way to think about it is to compare distances in the United States with others more familiar to you. For example:

New York to Washington, D.C., is about the same as:
    London to Paris
    Nairobi to Mombasa
    Tokyo to Kyoto
New York to Los Angeles is farther than:
    Lisbon to Cairo
    Moscow to Montreal
    New Delhi to Rome
New York to Chicago is close in distance to that between:
    Manila and Hong Kong
    Berlin and London
    Buenos Aires and Asunción

It is difficult for those people who come from smaller countries to realize what a factor this matter of sheer size is in the life of the United States. Not only is the country vast in extent; it also contains 204.6 million people (1970 census). This affects every phase of life—not only creating a highly competitive internal market for goods—which gives rise to constant advertising—but also a far-flung and equally competitive political arena. Wide geographic differences make for profound differences in attitudes and values. A traditional New Englander, for example, is as different in point of view from a Texan as is a Portuguese from a Finn, or an Indonesian from a Korean. Marked differences in geography or weather and widely dispersed ethnic heritages naturally affect peoples' attitudes—but in the United States such differences occur within the same nation. An overseas visitor once remarked: "No wonder Americans talk so loud and move so fast; in a place that size you almost have to or you get lost in the shuffle."

Size always affects psychology, whether it be among individuals or nations.

TIME ZONES

Another way to comprehend the vastness of the continent's size is to be aware of the time changes that take place as one moves across it. There are four different time zones between the two coasts:

When it is 12:00 Noon Eastern Standard Time in New York, it is
11:00 A.M. Central Standard Time in Chicago,
10:00 A.M. Mountain Standard Time in Denver,
9:00 A.M. Pacific Standard Time in San Francisco.

Canada, being wider from east to west, adds two more time zones: Atlantic Standard Time for New Brunswick, Nova Scotia, and Quebec; Yukon Standard Time for its extreme western provinces.

Alaska (the forty-ninth state of the United States, but not adjoining) extends even farther west than Canada and adds an additional two time zones: Alaska Standard Time and Nome Standard Time.

Time zones circle the world, an hour apart from each other. There are 24 around the earth, based on the "meridians" (or longitude lines) which start at Zero Meridian, which passes through

Greenwich, England. The American continent is so wide that it encompasses *one third* of all these time zones.

Long ago mankind had to make an arbitrary decision regarding the world's Date Line. Where would it be? Geographers established it halfway around the world from Zero Meridian, that is, 12 hours away from Greenwich, on the 180th Meridian. Luckily for all of us, the line runs for the most part through the open Pacific—the most convenient spot it could be! East of this imaginary line, the calendar is a day earlier than points west of it. People coming to the United States from Asia will therefore add a day to their lives—until they go home again!

CLIMATE

Naturally, with such distances, the climate in the United States also covers great extremes. From New England and New York through Chicago and most of the Midwest and Northwest, temperatures vary from sub-zero in winter to the high 90's or over in summer (Fahrenheit). Clothes, too, therefore, must cover a wide range.

The South, Southwest, and California have a warmer year, though even these sections have occasional frosts and periods of moderate cold. Speaking generally, you should be alert to the fact that summers are likely to range from 70°F to 100°F (21°C to 35°C) and in many areas can be quite humid. However, air conditioning is so widespread that you can expect most buildings—even private homes—to be kept at more or less 70°F (21°C).

CLOTHES

Winter temperatures throughout much of the country range from 0°F (or below) to more or less 50°F (– 20°C to 10°C). One should be prepared for a good deal of wind. Fur or leather coats or coats with quilted or furlike linings are needed in many places because of the wind. There is often snow, but in most cities it is quickly cleared, even in the northernmost part of the country.

Since indoors, even in winter, buildings are likely to be kept at approximately 70°F, heavy woolen suits and clothes are not comfortable indoors. You will need lightweight wool for winter with additional sweaters, jackets, stoles, ponchos, or the like to put on or take off easily as you move from hot to cold, from air conditioning to steam heat, from outdoors to indoors. Those who come from hot climates will perhaps feel drafts quite readily at first, especially in country houses, and should be prepared with extra scarves, sweaters, or other easily removed clothing.

For much of the country and much of the year, you will need heavy *outdoor* clothing, including boots, overcoat, warm gloves, and hat. You can buy these garments here at reasonable prices. You will need a raincoat—the combination kind with removable zip-out lining is especially useful—to be worn during the four in-between months of spring and autumn (April-May and September-October).

Most boys in the United States wear long trousers (rather than shorts, which are worn primarily for sports occasions) from the time they are about six years old—often earlier. People in general like bright colors and patterns; dress is informal, even in the cities. Few women wear hats, for example, except for wind and cold or for really dressy occasions such as weddings. Dark business suits for men and short cocktail dresses or dressy pantsuits for women suffice at most evening functions. People rarely "dress" for the theater except on Opening Nights; if "dress" is required at someone's home, you will be told "Black Tie." This, too, is rare, even in key cities.

Children dress very casually. They usually wear simple, "drip-dry" or "perma-prest" play clothes except for special occasions when they are dressed in "party clothes." In some parochial schools and a small number of private schools, uniforms are required, but this is unusual. Boys and girls generally wear a variety of sturdy and simple clothes to school, often jeans or corduroy slacks. A few schools still require jackets and ties, for boys, but the trend for young people is increasingly individualistic—even bizarre. Dress-up occasions can be quite competitive, ranging any-where from "doing your own thing" to ruffles and frills and starched collars, depending primarily on the geography. Speaking broadly, the South and Midwest tend to be more conventional than either coast.

Chapter 8

Moving Around Your New City

As is true throughout the world, you get yourself around a city on foot or by bus, taxi, your own car, or (in many cities) by subway.

ON FOOT

If distances are short or you need to go in two directions (east *and* west or north *and* south), by far the quickest way to go in most cases is on foot. Our needs are supplied in large measure by huge trucks and vans that converge on each town or city in the early morning, disgorge, and move out again. During working hours when these vehicles are unloading their massive piles of foodstuffs, clothes, raw materials, and other goods, street traffic can become so congested that it almost stops. Union regulations and the cost of overtime pay prevent such unloading being done at night, except under special circumstances. So people often get to their destination more quickly on foot than any other way.

BY BUS

Trams or trolley cars are now obsolete in most United States cities; generally the public travels by bus. More and more cities are requiring passengers to have the exact change in hand as they board the bus—or else "tokens" (small coinlike pieces similar to the French "jeton") that can be bought in advance. Labor here is so expensive that conductors were long ago taken off our buses. For some years drivers had the double job of making change at the same time that they were operating their monster buses through headlong traffic. This relatively new "exact change" rule eases the driver's load; it speeds service for everyone; it also reduces the number of robberies that were taking place when drivers had considerable extra money for making change.

In many cities bus and subway tokens can be used interchangeably, and are bought at subway booths. It is a great timesaver to buy tokens in considerable quantity and keep them in a special purse or envelope so that you can get at them easily. Otherwise you may have to wait on long lines in rush hour or get caught without change just when you need to catch a bus.

School children and people over sixty-five years of age can get special passes in most cities so that they can ride at reduced rates during certain hours of the day.

BY TAXI

Because at first they feel uncertain, most people are likely to travel by taxi when they arrive in any new place. Here taxis definitely come under the heading of "luxury" travel. In New York, for example, the meter reads sixty cents before you even move! Furthermore, taxis have an aggravating way of being hard to find not only at the busy hours of a day but also if the weather turns bad!

In some cities you can telephone to call them (see local phone book for numbers) but in others, including New York, you hail them on the street or find them at a hack stand.

Generally speaking, taxis are metered throughout the country, but there are some cities (for example, Washington, D.C.) where they operate on a distance zone system.

If you find yourself sharing a cab with several strangers (legal in some cities but not in others), you will often be expected to pay a full share, unfair though that may seem. In this diversified land where nothing is uniform, you will need to ask your fellow riders the custom; it varies from city to city.

Although drivers do not always comply, the rules are: they must stop if not showing an off-duty sign; they must drive anywhere within the city limits; they may not ask your destination before you get in and then refuse to take you; they may not charge more than is registered on the meter except for trunks, bridge, tunnel, or ferry tolls.

There are various sizes of cabs; often they are not permitted to carry more than four people—sometimes as few as three; some can carry five or six passengers.

In heavily congested areas the driver may not be allowed by law to get out of his cab to open doors or help with luggage. Do not assume he is being discourteous—it may be a safety measure.

If you want to make a complaint about taxi service, note the driver's number and name (posted on the dashboard); be sure to get the *name of the taxi company* also—there are many companies in all cities. When you write to the company, be sure to keep a copy of your letter.

BY SUBWAY

Subways are by far the quickest way to move about; networks of them underlie most major cities, operating day and night. Most of the time they are filled with people and can be used without a moment's hesitation. There are a few warnings, however, that should be observed:

1) Avoid rush hours if you can, as is true everywhere. Subways are crammed to breathless capacity from about 8:00 to 9:30 A.M. and again from about 4:30 to 6:00 or 6:30 P.M. (These are naturally the hours when pickpockets do their best work, too, as is true over most of the world.)

2) Don't travel by subway late in the evening, especially if you are not sure of the way. Corridors are dimly lit; unsavory people may lurk with intent to mug or steal. If it is late and the subway is quite empty, sit near the doors. Avoid the small seats in any empty train as these are easily blocked off.

3) Avoid weekend—especially Sunday—travel by subway if you can, except in well-traveled central areas of the city. Even in the daytime on weekends, subways are likely to be empty. When teenage "gangs" are bored and restless, they often roam about underground in search of trouble!

4) Hold your pocketbook firmly and consciously—don't let it dangle.

5) Be sure to buy tokens in quantity if you plan to use subways regularly.

YOUR OWN CAR

Costs

Owning a car in any U.S. city is expensive. In addition to the original cost of the car, one has to pay heavy insurance premiums. Rates vary by city and by coverage, but one can pay as much as $500 in insurance alone in congested cities.

In addition, the car must be licensed (fee depends on the weight of the car, but ranges from $10 to $50 or more); the cost of a driver's license must be added to that. All car licenses and fees are rising in cost as states add taxes to the automotive world.

There are no Customs or other duty charges on a private imported car if it is shipped home again within one year; however, if you sell it in the United States within a year, you will have to pay duty—6.5 percent of the appraised value of the car at the time of import (as of this writing). Be *sure* to bring your registration papers or proof of ownership. This is very important. Check with your nearest U.S. Consulate on latest rulings and charges before you come, or else with your local automobile club.

Licensing

It is recommended that you get an international registration marker for your car before leaving home. You will be allowed to drive to your destination with your national license plates or tags, but immediately on arrival you must obtain American license plates from the state in which you will be living. Each state has its own Department of Motor Vehicles which issues forms (see telephone directory for address) for both license and registration. Motorists will have to take a test and secure a U.S. driver's license unless they come from a country which is party to the International Convention on Road Traffic (1949) or the Inter-American Convention (1943), in which case they must carry an international driving permit. (See Appendix, Part III for list of countries in this category.)

Age minimums for the driver's license vary somewhat by state in the United States, but generally it is sixteen years of age or over. Driver training schools are found almost everywhere; it is good to have at least a few lessons of professional instruction *no matter how well you drive.* You will learn the rules of the road, local requirements, and especially the American "driving psychology." This varies considerably from country to country—a Frenchman, a Greek, a Japanese, and a Briton are all different behind the wheel!

Each state Motor Vehicle Bureau will give you a free booklet on request covering local rules. It is important to remember *ignorance of the law is never considered an excuse* if you run into trouble. You are expected to learn the law and abide by it when you drive.

Automobile Insurance

It is imperative to protect yourself adequately with liability insurance (covering damage to the other person). A few states have not yet made it compulsory, but you should insure yourself at a good substantial level, not the minimum. If you should hit anyone, damages charged here can be astronomically high. Lawyers assume that insurance companies (not the individual) will pay so they set damage fees accordingly. If you are *not* covered, you can be financially ruined by gigantic fees charged for injury, fright, shock, or other complaints—even if the accident appeared to you to be slight. Not everyone presses such suits, but enough people do so that you need to be well protected.

Buying a Car

Barring any strikes or emergency delays, you receive delivery on a new car quite quickly in this country. Most automobiles have greater horsepower than those sold abroad; most get fewer miles per gallon of gasoline (petrol). If you expect to do a great deal of long-distance driving, you probably would do well to purchase one of the heavier cars with a stronger engine. However, if you will just be doing short local driving, you will probably want to buy a "compact" or a foreign make of car. Most cities now have garages familiar with foreign cars which stock foreign spare parts, but it is advisable to look into this question of repairs before buying.

Don't buy a car at what is called "List Price" until you have talked to a number of people about it. Prices can usually be bargained down and can vary as much as 25 percent; prices also vary markedly from one month to another depending on how near the time is to the appearance of new models. Sometimes dealers then try to get rid of last year's model, and one can get a superb bargain as a result. Ask and explore; don't buy too fast.

Car dealers make their greatest profit in two ways: 1) on extras and 2) on arranging the financing and insurance. Let us look at both of these points:

Extras. These are the multitude of "optional" features which all dealers try hard to sell: radios or record players; special paint color; air conditioning; fancy seat covers; heaters or fans that are other than standard. Dealers are skilled at selling these items, but *you do not need to buy them.* If you are persuaded by a clever talker, it may cost you a considerable amount of extra money.

Financing and Insuring. Dealers normally charge higher interest rates than banks when they arrange the terms of financing—about .75 percent. Over the months or years of payment, this mounts up to a considerable amount. Look into alternative possibilities *before* you go to buy. Generally, you will do better to take out a bank loan rather than work through a car dealer—after all, he must take his

share and then he, too, will be working with a bank. He will do his
best to persuade you to finance the car through him, but it is not required. Don't feel obligated.

Secondhand Cars

The drop in price after one year or two is so great that many people always buy a used car rather than a new one. Prices vary depending on the age of the car, its condition, its size and make, the
locality of the country where it is bought, and the time of year.

Rule #1: in buying a secondhand car, don't even consider
buying one that is older than four years;

Rule #2: never go alone.Take someone with you who not only
knows cars well, but also knows the ways of American dealers.

Often it is an advantage to go to an area where wealthy people
live to find your car. They turn their cars in more often than poor
people and they normally take better care of them.

Used-car dealers vary widely as to reliability; try to deal with
one that has been recommended as reliable. Generally speaking,
your chances will be better with a reputable dealer than at a "used
car lot" though you will see these in profusion outside most big cities.

Many people do their buying outside city limits for several reasons: 1) the dealer's reputation is more vulnerable in a small environment so he tends to be more careful than in the anonymity of a
large city; 2) one can avoid paying city sales taxes. In New York
City, for example, there is a 7 percent sales tax on the price of any
purchase. If you can avoid this by going outside the city, your sav-
ing will be considerable.

It takes time and trouble to buy a secondhand car. If you do not
have a friend or office colleague who knows cars well, take a garage
mechanic with you. It would be worth what you have to pay him
for his time. Many mechanics are glad to do such "consulting"
work after hours or on weekends. Determine his price with him in
advance.

Be sure you actually *drive* the car before buying. You will be allowed to try it. Take it immediately to a nearby garage and ask the mechanic to test it out and give you his opinion. There are certain key parts that will give him a quick idea of the car's general condition. It is worth paying up to $25 for a careful going-over by a mechanic whom you trust. Do this *before* you sign any papers. Before you buy any car—new or used—talk to people at your office or any friends you have made. There are various tricks of the trade that you should know.

Renting a Car

With street parking so difficult, parking rates so high, and streets so crowded, increasing numbers of city dwellers are giving up the frustration of owning a car in the city. Instead, they are using public transportation for everyday use and renting cars only when they need them for out-of-town trips or vacations. Most overseas visitors are likely to find this by far the cheapest and easiest method too. There are many rental companies everywhere. As is true throughout the world, one can rent by the day, week, month, or year.

Your own firm may have a special discount arrangement with a particular rental agency—companies often do. It is worth asking about this at work. Some agencies have had bad experiences and will not rent to people from abroad because of past insurance difficulties or problems regarding payments. On the other hand, other agencies give additional discounts to visitors from abroad as a special courtesy. You will need to explore a bit and make inquiries for it all depends on what their past experience has been.

Costs are normally determined (as in other countries) by time-plus-mileage charges, with insurance and maintenance included in the basic rental cost. However, there is considerable variation: some include the gasoline, whereas others do not; some require that you return the car to its starting point, with others you can leave it in another city and return by some other means.

Theft of Cars and from Cars

Unfortunately, the stealing of cars is quite common. You have little comeback if your car was not locked or if the key was left in the ignition—even if the car *was* locked. The registration papers and your driver's license should be kept with you and not in the glove compartment where they would be convenient for the thief but not for you in trying to recover a stolen car! If you want to keep these papers in the car, be *sure* to have photocopies in a safe place at home as well.

Care should be taken regarding any possessions left in the car. If you must leave something—put it in the trunk or out of sight on the floor even if the car is locked. If traveling across the country in a loaded car, try to park it where you can see it when you stop for meals; at night take all visible items with you into your motel or hotel; put the rest in the locked trunk. Again this thievery is a part of the turmoil of our times, often resulting from the need for immediate cash for a quick "fix," that is, drugs.

Gasoline and Service Stations

Prices vary by state depending on local taxes. The cheapest variety of gasoline, called "Regular," is perfectly good for all except high-powered engines or very high altitudes.

The U.S. gallon is slightly smaller than the British "imperial gallon," approximately four liters according to the metric system.

One can order by asking for a specific number of gallons or by price ("$3 worth please") or just asking to have the tank "filled up." Most tanks hold about 16 to 18 gallons when full.

Routine free services which one can expect (or ask for) at service stations include: checking the oil, tires, and water in the battery; cleaning the windshield; use of their rest rooms (gas stations are the normal places to stop when on a long trip); and free road maps. One does not tip gas station attendants for any of these services.

If your engine is hot, the attendant should not be asked to check the water in your radiator and he may decline to do so. So many attendants have been badly burned by gushing steam that this is no longer a regular service—as it used to be.

Traffic Rules

Cars travel on the right throughout the United States; one must by law signal not only for all turns but also for changes of lane. Traffic laws are being enforced more and more strictly as congestion problems grow ever more acute in American cities. Police may travel in unmarked cars; speed regulations are often checked by radar.

If you hear the sirens of fire trucks, ambulances, or police cars approaching, *immediately* pull over to the right and stop or slow down to let them pass.

Horn-blowing is not allowed in most cities; don't try to move traffic along by using your horn. You could be fined.

If you come to a yellow school bus at a standstill—even if it has stopped on the opposite side of the road—*stop your car.* This law is strictly enforced because children may be running across the road to or from the bus.

Never stop your car on a highway. If you have a problem or want to read a map or change drivers, drive it (or push it) well to the side of the road. Speeds on our highways are such that a stopped car is extremely dangerous, for oncoming drivers cannot see that it is stationary until they are almost on top of it.

Never pass on a curve or near the top of a hill; don't ever cross yellow or solid white lines. These are among the most common offenses for which police are on the lookout; they are also alert for anyone going through a red light or a Stop sign at an intersection. One can be stopped and fined for any of these faults.

Traffic lights are controlled for different speeds; in large cities these vary depending on the area, flow of traffic, and time of day. Often they are set for 25 miles per hour. If you try to find and maintain the set speed, you will "make" most lights and "flow" with the traffic. Talk to taxi drivers about this. They are experts at "making lights" and can give you many tips.

Speed Limits

Speed limits are strictly enforced, sometimes by radar, sometimes by unmarked police cars, sometimes by regular police cars which radio to one another up and down the highways.

Watch all road signs carefully as you drive along. Speed regulations change frequently at various locations; *do what they say.* They may decrease suddenly, for example, at the approach to a small town or built-up area, a factory roadway, or a railroad. They are particularly enforced in school traffic zones, which extend on either side of any school and are posted as "School Zone." This is usually a 15-mile-per-hour area; it is essential to reduce speed drastically in such zones. Even small children cross the road by themselves; they play with balls and bicycles along the edge of the road and can be a really dangerous hazard.

Rules for People on Foot

Jaywalking—which means crossing anywhere except at the corner or crossing against the traffic light—is an offense. You can be fined rather heavily if caught. You will see many people taking chances, but do not follow their example. It is not worth it. Most pedestrian injuries are the result of one or the other offense.

If you come from a left-hand drive country, be especially careful to look *both* ways for oncoming cars and have your children practice doing the same. Many people are hurt by failing to do this before stepping off the curb.

Parking Rules

When you park a car, read the signs carefully. They vary in different parts of the city, at different times of the day, on different days of the week. The only way you can know what is legal for that particular spot is to read the sign. There are no blue disk zones in

the United States. Many cars are towed away each day by city police for parking violations. As cities get more crowded, this procedure is spreading and being more and more effectively carried out.
It is not worth the risk. You pay for the towaway; expenses for actually retrieving the car are high; in addition you pay a heavy penalty fine. The whole thing can add up to $75! In addition you go
through endless red tape, embarrassment, and inconvenience. Be
careful not to park near fire hydrants, bus stops, private driveways,
or too near the corners of blocks. Towaways can result from any of
these parking violations as well as for being in a "No Parking"
area.

The following are some familiar parking rules:

"No Stopping"	This means what it says: you cannot park *or even stop.*
"No Parking"	Here you may stop long enough to pick up or discharge passengers or to drop off merchandise; you can stop your car for a brief time if someone is in the driver's seat and able to move the car if necessary.
"No Standing"	You may only drop people off or pick them up if you can do it quickly; you cannot wait until they come and you cannot leave the car there while you go in to deliver a parcel or message.
Fire Hydrants	The rule is: no standing or parking within 15 feet.
Bus Stops and Taxi Stands	If you do not interfere with traffic you can pause in them briefly, but you cannot get out of the car; you must be alert to move at a moment's notice.
Hitchhikers	You will often see young people or sol- diers "thumbing" a ride, especially along the main highways. *Do not* stop

for them. Unfortunately, this practice can be quite dangerous as they may not be as innocent as they look. Furthermore, in many states, it is as illegal to pick up a person as to ask for rides. You could be fined quite heavily and lose your insurance for doing it.

$$ and Sense

American money can be quite confusing. The bills—or paper money—are all the same color and size. One has to look carefully to be sure he is giving out a $1 bill and not a $10 bill, for example. Furthermore, new bills stick together easily. Be sure this does not happen to you.

Coins are also confusing. This is partly because some of them have two names; partly because the size does not indicate the value. The ten-cent coin is smaller than the five-cent coin, for example. In addition all coins are silver-colored except for the penny (one cent) which is copper-colored.

COINS

1¢—penny or cent   The coin of smallest value, equal to 1/100 of a dollar. It is useful for parking meters or to pay sales tax in stores, but one of them does not buy very much! Five pennies equal one nickel.

5¢—nickel   Large; easily confused with the quarter.

10¢—dime   Smallest of the coins, but one of the most useful. It is used for pay telephones, buying newspapers, coin-operated machines, and some bus fares.

25¢—quarter   This coin is larger than the nickel but easy to mistake for it. This is the normal tipping coin; also commonly used for paying bridge and road tolls.

One has to keep considerable change on hand, especially in cities which require exact change for their buses. Sales taxes also require a lot of small coins, although stores will make change. Bus drivers, however, are often not allowed to make change in many cities.

BILLS

These come in the following denominations: $1, $5, $10, and $20.
They also come in $50 and $100 bills, but these are seen less often by most of us! Keep small-value bills with you. Taxi drivers, subway attendants, and some store clerks will not change anything larger than a $5 bill; most supermarket check-outs will however.

It is a good idea to get a selection of American coins and bills from your bank before leaving home and practice with them so that you can recognize them easily. If you do this with your children too, they can also become comfortable with the currency and make that adjustment before they even arrive.

There is no limit to the dollars you can bring into or take out of the United States; however, your own country may, of course, have its restrictions about the amount you may take with you. You will need to check on that before leaving home.

MONEY ON ARRIVAL

You will need a *minimum* of $25 of American money on arrival at a U.S. airport for tips to porters and for transportation into the city. There are money exchanges in all international airports, but it is a bother to stop at the moment of arrival when one also has to cope with luggage, crowds, fatigue, and so forth. It is better to convert an adequate supply of money before departing. Taxi fares are rising rapidly in this country (about $12 to get into New York City from Kennedy Airport, for example). Airports are likely to be several miles out from most cities. Airport buses are *much* less expensive and are recommended unless you have a large number of people in your group or considerable luggage. The bus will take you to a central point in the city from where you can hire a cab to your final destination at far lower cost.

BANKS

Before you open a checking account, ask carefully about the various possible plans. A "Regular" account requires a specific (rather high) balance in the bank at all times, but there is no charge for each check issued. A "Special" account does not require as large a balance, but there is a charge for each check and sometimes a small monthly carrying charge as well.

Unless you use 20 to 25 checks each month, a "Regular" account is not worthwhile. You would do better to put the large balance required into a savings bank and draw interest on it. (*NOTE:* Savings banks generally pay approximately 1 percent more interest than do commercial banks so they are better places to keep any sizable amounts of money.)

The United States is becoming more and more a "cashless society"; people are making purchases by check or charge account or credit card, rather than by carrying a good deal of money in their pockets or purses.

Normally people pay by check at the end of each month at department stores and some supermarkets and drugstores; they also pay monthly by check for rent, telephone, electricity, milk, newspaper delivery, and similar household expenses; many have charge cards to pay for gasoline and service station expenses and credit cards for restaurant, hotel, and travel costs.

Many other people, however, prefer to "pay-as-they-go" and not to accumulate monthly bills. Most people work out a combination, paying some bills in cash and charging others. This is a matter of personal choice. But if you have charge accounts, be *sure* to pay promptly; the overcharges for late payments can be high. Once you are recognized or have opened an account, you can use checks instead of cash at most stores.

However much money you keep on your premises or in your pocket or purse, you should be extremely careful with it. Never leave a wallet or purse on a desk in your office or on a store counter *for even a moment.* Keep them out of sight and away from the entrance hall or doorway even at home; do not carry too much cash when you go out. Regretfully, purse-snatching and pocket-picking are quite common in metropolitan areas in the United States, as they are in other parts of the world too.

SAFE DEPOSIT BOXES

If you have jewelry or other valuables (passports, wills, stock certificates, mortgage or insurance papers, leases, and so on), you should rent a safe deposit box at a nearby bank. This will cost between $7 and $55 per year depending on the size of the box and the area of the country. You can get your valuables out any time within banking hours, but these irreplaceable items will be safe and protected in the bank vaults. If you are staying in a hotel, have the desk clerk put jewelry and other items into the hotel safe. *Do not leave* valuables in your hotel room, even in a suitcase. Insure jewelry, furs, expensive cameras, watches, or any items that can easily be stolen. It is worth it.

SENDING MONEY ABROAD

There are several ways to send money to someone in another country. If time is important, you may make arrangements at your bank by asking them to send a "cable transfer" to a bank in another country. If there is no urgency, banks can make less expensive transfers by letters to foreign banks. If you want the bank to notify the receiver of the funds, be sure to tell them the person's address! In order to receive such funds, the person will have to present himself at the overseas bank with proper identification.

Money can also be sent abroad through the U.S. Postal Service. (See Chapter 12.)

CHARGE ACCOUNTS AND CREDIT CARDS

Most department stores offer charge accounts; they will ask for bank and other credit references when you apply. The process of opening an account may take a week or more. You will be given a "charge card" when your application is approved. This makes it possible to charge purchases and minimizes the amount of cash you have to carry with you; it greatly speeds up the buying process; you can return goods and obtain a credit on your account. You generally will not get a cash refund, but your account will be credited.

The *disadvantage* of a charge account is that one must be *very* careful about the charge card. If you lose it and someone picks it up, he can run up heavy charges on your account, yet you will be held liable until you cancel the card. If you *do* lose it, call the store *immediately* and report the loss; then *write them at once* and report it again in writing, telling them the day and hour when you phoned in to report the loss. Keep a copy of the letter. You will not be liable *after the time you first reported it.* Carry your charge cards with you only when you plan to go shopping—do not normally carry them in your purse or wallet.

Some people leave them at home, making a note of the account number. This is safer but slower, for then the salesclerk must check your number, by telephone, with each purchase. This often takes quite a while, and the waiting can be tedious.

TIPPING

This is a difficult subject. There are no absolute rules; most people vary between 15 and 20 percent depending on how much service they have had, how many people have been involved, how long they have been at a place, how much they enjoyed it, and where they were in the United States.

Fifteen percent (in big cities) indicates minimal satisfaction; 20 percent means something a bit more than that. Outside major cities, 15 percent is still the common tip.
The normal tipping coin for small services is the quarter (25¢).

People you DO tip in the United States are:

Waiters, taxi drivers, porters, doormen, hat-check girls; you also tip for personal services such as: barbers, shoeshine boys, beauty parlor attendants, and so on.

People you DO NOT tip include:

Customs officials or *other government employees* such as policemen or firemen. This is considered bribery.
Mailmen. You do not tip them, but you do give them a Christmas gift of $2 to $3 each (there may be several serving a large apartment house).
Airline personnel. No tips to stewards, stewardesses, or ticket agents.
Room clerks or *people at hotel desks.* (Not like the European concierge system.)
Bus drivers. Except if they also serve as guides on guided tours—then give them $1 with a "Thank you" as you leave.
Store clerks.
Gas station attendants.
Elevator operators, receptionists, or *telephone girls.*
Employees in clubs.
Theater ushers or *movie ushers.* Programs are also free (paid for by the advertisements in them). You *do,* however, tip ushers at sports events, for some unknown reason, and you *do* pay for sports programs.
Generally speaking: If in doubt as to whether or not to tip, err on the side of giving rather than not giving. Unfortunately, tipping is a prevalent custom in the United States.

Normal Tips

There is disagreement about amounts, and tipping customs vary considerably from one part of the United States to another, as well as from small town to large city. When you are settled in your area, you should ask about this locally.

But to put newcomers at ease during their initial few days, the following suggestions are offered:

Waiters

Give at least 15 percent to the waiter. Tips are *not included* in our bills. Give the waiter more if you have asked for extras, been particularly slow, had a large group, or requested help in understanding the menu or in serving young children—that is, if he has given more than minimal service in any way.

As everywhere, tips are naturally higher in fancier restaurants. If you order wine, the wine steward may expect a tip as well as the waiter. In such a place your tip for the waiter should be not less than 20 percent.

In a low-priced restaurant, snack bar, or coffeehouse, the tip is about 25¢ for a bill of $1.25. Leave 15 to 25¢ under your plate for anything less than that. If you have just had a single cup of coffee or tea, you can leave a dime (10¢).

If you order room service in a hotel, the minimum tip is 25¢; 20 percent of the bill is proper above that.

Taxi Drivers

A quarter is enough for any fare up to $1.50; after that, give 15–20 percent. If the ride is less than 75¢, you can give 15¢ (this is rare nowadays!). If there are several people or you have a lot of luggage, give a little more. In some cities (as in Atlanta) there is an extra charge for each passenger. Such variations are posted in the cab so you can read them.

Porters

Many air, bus, or rail terminals now charge a fixed fee of 35¢ a
bag. If they do, this information is posted. Otherwise, 25¢ a bag or
50¢ for a small trunk is adequate.

Doormen

For normal small daily services, you do not tip *except* if they call
a taxicab. Then give them a quarter. If they help with a great deal
of luggage at any time, give them 25–50¢, depending on the amount
of trouble taken.

Most people give doormen occasional tips—ranging from 50¢ to
$2—for any extra services they may perform or on special occa-
sions such as Easter or if they have given (and have not been tipped
for) a good many small services over a considerable period of time.
This is considered a "sweetener." It is not required, but it helps to
keep service amiable and good!

Christmas

Christmas is special and expensive!

If you live in an apartment house where there are doormen, give
each one of them a gift of $5 or more at Christmastime. The
amount will vary depending on how long you have been living
there, the size of your family, and how many other tips you have
given throughout the year. At Christmas also the superintendent of
your apartment house should be given a gift of $15 or more.

Christmas tips are normally given also to the tradespeople one
sees regularly—the laundryman, newspaper boy, milkman, parking
lot attendant, hairdresser or barber. There is some leeway depending on how often they have served you, how friendly you are together, and your own financial level. But if you feel warmly dis-
posed to them, $2 to $5 in a Christmas card would be much
appreciated by any or all such people who have worked for you
throughout the year.

Personal Services

Barber.	40–50¢ in New York; less in smaller cities.
Shoeshine boy.	15¢ in New York (on a 35¢ shoeshine).
Hat-check attendant.	25¢ normally; more for a long period or a fancy place, or a very late hour.
Hairdresser.	20 percent of the bill normally; the one who does the washing, 35–50¢; manicurist, 35–50¢.
Parcel delivery boy.	15–25¢ depending on size and weight of delivery.
Parking lot attendant.	25¢ only if they park and bring your car; do not tip if you park your own car.
Hotel Chambermaid.	3 days or less, 50¢ to $1 a night; over 3 days, $2 a week (more if there are children or special services).

Chapter 10

To Your Good Health

FINDING A DOCTOR

One of the first things you will need to do when you settle into your house or apartment is to find a doctor and get on his "list." This should be done *before* you or anyone in your family needs his services. Doctors in this country are so busy that all too often people have real trouble in getting help when they need it if they have not made a prior connection with a physician. You may be lucky enough to find someone who will see you at a moment's notice, but a doctor's first obligation is to his own patients. If he is very busy, a newcomer who is not on his list may have to wait a good while. It is far better to become one of his patients before any crisis arises.

General practitioners—or "family doctors"—are becoming increasingly rare; as medicine gets more and more complicated, doctors tend more and more to specialties. Those physicians known as "internists"—meaning internal ailments—are now taking the place of family doctors in many areas. If your trouble falls into some other category, the doctor will refer you to the proper specialist and make the connection for you.

How do you go about finding a reliable doctor whom you can afford? It is not easy, and it usually takes a bit of time. Don't necessarily accept the first physician suggested. People have different needs. Do you care most about top-level technical competence? Or is it important to you for your doctor to have a gentle personality and to be willing to give you considerable time? Are costs of primary importance to you, or is it vital that the doctor come to the house? (By no means will all doctors do this—it too is becoming increasingly rare in this country.)

There are a variety of ways to search. Your company may advise you. Often there is a company doctor or they may have connections with a medical "group." This is a great help. Perhaps you will ask your neighbors or the person from whom you rent your apartment, or the head of your child's school. The officer at the bank or your church minister may also give you advice as to someone you can trust. Your own consulate may have a list of doctors who speak your language.

Failing a personal recommendation from someone you know, go to the local library and ask for the *Directory of Medical Specialists.* Look up your city or area in it, and there find an internist whose age, medical training, and background seem right to you. Then make an appointment to see him. Take him your family's health records and ask about his range of fees, his hospital connections, whether or not he makes house visits, and anything else you want to know. This is your chance to decide about him; it is the time he gets to know you and your needs. He will, of course, bill you for the time spent, but it is worth it.

If such an approach seems unsatisfactory to you, you can call the administrator's office at the nearest hospital. Ask the secretary to tell you the office addresses of two or three of the newest internists who have been given "privileges" at that hospital. This way you will find well-trained men with a nearby hospital affiliation. If they are either young or new to the neighborhood, they are probably not yet swamped with more patients than they can handle so they will be able to take on a new family.

Another approach is to go in person to the local hospital's Emergency Room. The residents on duty there know very well who the good internists are for they watch them in action under trying circumstances. They know the good from the bad, the kindly from the brusque, the thorough from the superficial.

In America, hospitals are the best criteria for continued medical competence. If a doctor is on the staff of a really good hospital, he is under pressure to keep his medical knowledge and ability up to date; therefore you can place your confidence in him.

Don't feel shy about discussing fees when you first make these contacts. They vary widely and it is better to know in advance the range of price for any given physician.

As we have said before, be braced for high costs, especially in large cities where high overhead is passed on to the patients in doctors' bills.

General Advice

For routine family medical care, look for a young man who has had good medical training but has not had the time to develop an overheavy work load. He will probably give you more attention and charge less. If the problem is technically difficult, you (or he) can and will consult a specialist anyway.

EMERGENCIES

If an emergency strikes and you have no doctor—or the one you have is unobtainable—take the patient yourself by car or taxi directly to the Emergency Ward of the nearest hospital. It is a good idea to make a mental note of where this is almost as soon as you arrive. Some people post a note by their telephone listing emergency addresses and telephone numbers so that in the confusion of an accident they can save the time of searching frantically for such essential information.

If you cannot move the patient or if the situation is one in which time is essential, lift the telephone receiver and simply say to the operator: "I need an ambulance; please contact the police." If you do this, *do not forget to give your address.* Many a person has hung up without doing this and thereby wasted precious moments while the operator has had to call back—and sometimes been unable to trace the call.

IF YOU ARE SENT TO A HOSPITAL

Although health care is unbelievably expensive in the United States, it is good and in most cases very thorough. People are sent to hospitals more often here than in many other countries. If this happens to you, don't fear the worst! It often only means that the doctor wants to make use of special facilities for tests, X-ray, or treatment procedures or that he wants to have you observed at frequent intervals over a period of days by a trained staff. Don't be frightened! It does not necessarily mean that he thinks you are seriously ill.

HEALTH INSURANCE

Since medical costs are so high, insurance is *necessary*. There are many excellent free public facilities for the poor, but they are so crowded and the waiting time is so long that most people who can afford it use private medicine. As yet there is no national system of health insurance like those in many other countries of the world (except for Medicare which covers only persons over 65 years of age).

In lieu of this, the great majority of the American people subscribe to *private* insurance programs which help to pay for hospital and doctor bills. You should join such a program too. If you work for an American enterprise, it is quite likely that there is a group insurance plan to which you and your family will automatically belong, but you should find out about this in detail. If there is such a plan, payments are made through automatic payroll deductions. Find out exactly what the coverage includes since this varies from one plan to another. Is maternity care included? What about dental coverage? surgery? eye care? pediatrics?

If you are working for an organization which does not have group insurance, you *most certainly* should purchase private health insurance for yourself and your family. One bad accident could cost you more than you own. Most insurance plans are open to international personnel after they have been U.S. residents for six months; a few will cover them earlier than that.

Foreign students enrolled in U.S. colleges and universities pay their college infirmary fee and are entitled to receive infirmary care whenever they need it. They can also purchase additional low-cost accident insurance—which is advised. The university or college catalogue will give details. Families of students, however, are *not* eligible for infirmary care and should be covered with outside health insurance.

Not all medical expenses will be covered by any insurance. Read the policy carefully and have someone explain it to you in detail. Coverage varies widely from one policy to another. Usually they do *not* include drugs and medicines, dental care, eyeglasses, or doctors' visits to the home. You can have these specialties added, but the cost rises sharply with each one. Be sure to think over carefully exactly what you really need, balancing the cost of the policy against those services you could afford to cover yourself.

Before selecting a health insurance agent, it is a good idea to obtain advice from a colleague or friend. Most agents are reliable, but some are not; you will need help in selecting a reputable firm.

Paying Hospital Bills

Be prepared to pay all hospital bills before taking the patient home. Your corporation or your insurance may cover such matters for you; otherwise the hospital is likely to demand full payment— even if this requires your taking out a loan to cover it. It is advisable to talk to your employer, your doctor, or your insurance agent about this so you will know your own situation before an emergency arises.

BEFORE YOU LEAVE HOME

Bring your family's health records with you if you can. This may save on expensive tests or background studies. Also, have full dental attention before you leave home; costs for dentistry as well as medical care are extremely high in the United States.

If you wear eyeglasses, have an extra pair with you, and be sure to bring a copy of the prescription.

Chapter 11

Food and Food Customs

HOTELS

Most people start their visit to the United States by staying in a hotel. You will find that hotel restaurants, grills, lounges, and so on, are nearly always more expensive than neighborhood restaurants; in addition, hotel food is often not especially good and hotel dining rooms are sometimes dull. It is worth wandering up and down the nearby streets to see if you cannot find something less expensive and more fun. The words "coffee shop" in a hotel (or airport) means that prices are more reasonable than in a restaurant; "snack bars" are even cheaper, but you may have to stand at the counter or sit in a booth.

RESTAURANTS

Because America is home to so many different nationalities, one can find almost any kind of restaurant in practically all the larger cities. Listings in the classified telephone directory may be by nationality or by area of the city or both; they range widely in price. Many post their menus in the window so you can get an idea of prices before you enter. If not, you may want to ask to see a menu before you get really settled, or else just ask about the price range. Appearances from the outside can be deceptive as to price—what looks small and inconspicuous may turn out to be very expensive, or a nice-looking place may be quite moderate. It works both ways.

You can get a solid meal for about $2 or slightly more if you eat in snack bars, chain restaurants, or drugstores, but in a medium-priced city restaurant you should expect to pay $6 to $8 per person for a nicely served dinner—with wine or drinks extra. Prices in New York City go "upward" fast!

RESERVATIONS

If you are going to a middle- or upper-level restaurant to dine, telephone ahead for a reservation—the earlier the better. Keep to the time you have given or else phone to say you will be late. Cities are crowded, and good restaurants will not hold reservations for more than a short time. If you are turned away because you have not reserved ahead, don't take it personally. It happens all the time. The management has no choice. Fire laws are extremely strict about the number of occupants; unannounced fire inspections are frequent. No restaurateur dares overcrowd his establishment.

CAFETERIAS—LUNCH COUNTERS—DINERS

These are quick and cheap; the food and handling are inspected regularly by government officials so you can feel safe, although you are advised to choose a clean-looking place nonetheless. These "quickies" are crowded with people at normal mealtimes, but if you eat a little early or a little late, you can usually get a seat without waiting too long. They abound everywhere, are open long hours, and are useful in keeping your food budget down.

Diners—which look somewhat like railroad cars—are often found on the outskirts of towns; they vary from clean and shiny to rather bedraggled. Truck drivers often stop at them because they are apt to have good parking facilities; many motorists do too. Diners serve large portions of good, filling food at low prices; furthermore, there is often an interesting cross section of people in them, especially in the early morning hours when the long-distance truck drivers are eating breakfast.

You do not generally tip at cafeterias where you serve yourself; nor is tipping required at a lunch counter, although most people leave some small change under their plate when they leave.

DRUGSTORES

Far into the night, you can sit at a counter in a drugstore and get coffee, tea, or cocoa, sandwiches, soups, ice cream, soft drinks, and sometimes hamburgers or hot dogs. Most of them do not serve real meals, although some do.

BARS

American bars are less full of camaraderie than are bars in many other countries—no dart throwing or other games; rarely a pretty barmaid; people seldom toast each other or offer a "drink all around." U.S. bars are more often dark, quite dismally dignified.

It is a good idea to name your brand of alcohol if you care about this. Otherwise you are likely to get a cheap "house" brand.

Don't order beer by the "pint" or "half pint." Ask for a glass (usually 8 to 10 ounces) or a bottle. American beer is usually light and served very cold. Imported beers, mostly European, are generally available also. Japanese beer is beginning to appear in the main cities.

U.S. whiskey tends to be sweeter, more full-bodied, and cheaper than the whiskeys of Scotland or Ireland; Canadian whiskey is light. The main U.S. whiskeys are bourbon (made from corn) or a blend of several grains incorrectly called "rye" or simply called "blended whiskey." If you want the real "rye," be sure the bartender understands. He will generally serve the mixture unless you make your desire clear.

If you like your drink at room temperature, be sure to say "no ice." Americans like most of their drinks ice cold.

HOURS OF MEALS

It is possible to be served a meal at any hour—including all night—in most large cities. Many restaurants close on Sunday, but many others are open. Chains such as Horn and Hardart, Schrafft, and Howard Johnson are found in the telephone book; these usually list certain locations which are open on Sunday.

Some places offer Sunday "Brunch" (or you might be invited to a "Brunch" at someone's house). This is a combination of breakfast and lunch, served about 11:30 or twelve o'clock for late Sunday sleepers.

If you are outside a major city, it may be difficult to find a place that is open after 8:30 or 9:00 P.M., though lunch counters, "diners," and drugstores usually stay open late.

In people's homes there is considerable variety as to eating times. Around cities the main meal is usually served in the evening, but in rural areas it may be eaten in the middle of the day. In commuting areas, dinner is often quite late because of train schedules. In cities people normally eat dinner about 7:00 or 7:30 if they have cocktails, earlier if they do not. Throughout the country most people dine relatively early—6:30 P.M. is quite common; the hour for parties is usually later.

FIND OUT WHERE TO GO

Most cities feature a multitude of inexpensive paperback books covering their eating places; local magazines and newspapers carry advertisements; there are lists of national restaurants which run the gamut of price and elegance. The best thing to do is to browse in the local bookstore, to find a book which indicates price ranges, and then go explore! Your colleagues at work will be glad to offer suggestions too, both pro and con.

AMERICAN FOOD HABITS

Generally speaking, American food is rather bland and unspiced; salads are much liked and are served all year round. Many people in this sedentary country are trying to keep down their weight and so they are "calorie" conscious. This is evident in menus offering "low calorie" or "weight watchers" meals. In markets one can find "No Cal" drinks (meaning without calories) such as ginger ale or cola; "diet" foods without sugar or salt are also available in food stores. You need not bother with these shelves, but you may be interested in knowing they are there!

Waiters in restaurants tend to assume that everyone drinks coffee, but you do not have to do so! If he suddenly says "Now or later?" what he means is "Do you want coffee with your meal or later?" Many—but by no means all—Americans drink coffee or tea *with* their meal. Either way is perfectly acceptable. When dining out, you can ask for tea, milk, Coke, beer, and so on, if you prefer these to coffee; normally when eating in a home it is considered better manners to take whatever is being served and not to ask for something different—unless the hostess gives you a choice. Restaurants cannot serve beer, wine, or liquor unless they are licensed to do so.

The main course in American meals is usually meat, fowl, or fish, but rarely is more than one of these served at the same meal (except that seafood can be used as an appetizer—shrimp cocktail, pickled herring, oysters, etc.).

Most North Americans eat quickly during the day—that is, breakfast and lunch—unless it is a social, business, or family occasion. The evening meal, however, is usually leisurely and a family time. Racing through daytime meals is part of the "pace" described earlier; working time is considered precious. There is also another reason—namely, the ever-present pressure of numbers. People in public eating places are waiting for you to finish so they too can be served and get back to work within the allotted time. So each one hurries to make room for the next person.

There is a real difference in leisure and timing here when a meal is "social," meaning shared and enjoyed, or when it is "just a meal."

A LANGUAGE ALL ITS OWN

Meat

If you order steaks, chops, hamburgers, and so on, the waiter may look at you blankly and say: "How d'ya want it?" What he means is: rare? medium? well done?

"Rare" is likely to be *very* rare; "well done" to be very well done. If you prefer, you can indicate something in the middle by saying "medium rare" or "medium well done."

Coffee

If you are asked "Regular?" when you order, this means "Do you want lots of cream in it?" If not, ask for "black" (no cream) or "dark" (meaning a small amount of cream). Often the cream is brought separately, and you add your own—but not always.

Coffee is the usual American drink at all hours of the day. It varies enormously in quality; you will just have to experiment to find places that make it the way you like it. Espresso is often available, but one has to ask for it.

Tea

Tea is much less popular in the United States than coffee—perhaps because it is often quite poor (perhaps we make it poorly because we don't drink it as much as other nationalities do). In public places tea is usually a shock to the newcomer. A cup of hot water (no longer boiling if it ever was) is brought in with a limp tea bag in the saucer. You are supposed to put the bag into the water and leave it there until the tea is as strong as you like it. In private homes one will generally find it better made than this!

Other Drinks

Next after coffee, Americans are likely to drink Coke or other soft drinks, milk shakes or other milk drinks, or fruit juices. Iced tea is apt to be good and is widely drunk in summer, as is iced coffee. If you want to drink water, you will probably have to ask for it. It is safe anywhere.

Bread and Butter

These are usually served in restaurants whether or not you ask for them; there is no charge for them.

Eggs

Boiled eggs are broken into cups—rarely, if ever, eaten out of the shell; fried may be "sunny-side up," meaning fried on one side only (with the yellow face showing); "over," meaning well fried on both sides; or "over easy," meaning fried lightly on both sides.

The waiter at a restaurant will ask you: "How do you want your eggs?" Your answer can include any one of a wide range of possibilities: boiled, fried, scrambled, or poached; with or without ham or bacon or sausage. You also indicate the number of eggs you want. Many Americans consider two normal.

Additional prices for one or two slices of bacon or a sausage or two may be out of all proportion. Take a look at the price on the menu before ordering.

French Fries and "Slaw"

"French fries" are fried potatoes—like British "chips." You often get them with a meal whether you order them or not; the same is true of small paper cups of cole slaw—sliced cabbage and mayonnaise. If these are served with the meal, there is no extra charge for them.

Hot Dogs or "Franks"

Usually these are eaten in a long bread roll; they can be either beef or pork. You have your choice of adding tomato ketchup (spiced tomato sauce), mustard, pickle, relish, or onion (sliced and raw); some people put all of these on at once! There is no charge for such condiments.

The special language of the "short order" cook behind a lunch counter is a mystery even to Americans. Orders such as "draw one" or "shoot one" mean "pour a cup of coffee" or "pour a glass of Coke"; "B.L.T." means a "bacon, lettuce, and tomato" sandwich; if you hear "B.L.T. down," this means "on white toast"! You do not have to *know* this language, but it is amazing to listen to it as you sit at a busy counter. Feel free to *order* in normal terms however. The man serving you does not expect you to use his jargon!

Chapter 12

Getting in Touch with People

POSTAL SERVICE

Mail service in the United States is expensive, poor, and often incredibly slow, especially in the large cities, where millions of pieces are handled by antiquated equipment. Deliveries are made normally only once a day to private homes, twice to offices.

For ordinary mail within the United States, buy a "roll" of 100 of the required stamp (currently 8¢), plus a supply of air letter forms for overseas. If you have such supplies for your normal daily needs, you can then drop your letters into the nearest mailbox and avoid standing in long lines at the post office. If you must go to the post office, try to avoid the lunch hour or the four to five o'clock rush when every mailing clerk in the city is bringing in the day's office mail.

Sending Money Abroad

If you want to forward money by postal order, be sure to ask for an *international* form; many a person has mistakenly sent the domestic one which cannot be cashed abroad. You must specify this clearly.

Registry

If you want to be sure an important letter has been received, send it "Registered, with Return Receipt Requested."

Most personal mail goes first class. Other classes of mail cover advertisements, magazines, and so forth. If you are interested in anything besides the usual first class postage, ask at the post office for: "Special Delivery" (delivered by hand) or "Insured Mail" or rates on mailing "In Bulk."

Parcels

There are many rules and regulations governing the mailing of packages; permissible sizes and weights vary; some *must* be sealed, and others may not be sealed but *must* be tied with string (so they can be opened for inspection). You are advised to ask at the post office (by telephone if you like) before you wrap a parcel for shipment abroad so as to save yourself the nuisance of having to take it home and begin again.

Never include anything written in a package; if you get caught doing so, you can be fined. Written materials—even short notes—are supposed to go by the more expensive first class mail. If you want the note to arrive with the parcel, put it in an ordinary envelope with the proper first class stamp, fasten the envelope to the parcel with gummed tape or glue, and write clearly on it: "Letter Inside." The recipient will be sure to notice it then and not think it is merely a label.

There are special rates for books and printed matter. Ask the postal clerk about this.

TELEPHONES

The United States is a telephone land. Almost everyone uses the telephone to make or break social engagements, to say their "Thank you's," to do their shopping and ordering (even from food and drug stores), and to obtain all kinds of information. Telephones save your feet and endless amounts of time—not to mention multiple bus or subway fares! Do get used to using the phone readily. It is the chief means of communication in the United States. Some visitors from other countries hesitate at first either because it is unfamiliar or because they are afraid that they will be "intruding" or "bothering" the other person. Within normal hours —after eight in the morning and before nine at night (but not at mealtimes)—people are used to the telephone ringing and will not mind at all. All offices have an employee whose job it is to answer the phone. You need never worry about calling a business concern for information, nor will you find them closed at lunchtime, though of course a particular individual may be out.

It is simple and quick to have a phone installed. Just call the Business Office of the Telephone Company (see the Directory). They will install it on a specific day by appointment, when it is convenient for you. You must be at home to tell them where you want it placed. (All this is barring strikes or emergencies, of course.)

Although you will be offered a multitude of extra services and a variety of fancy phones, just ask for the basic installation. Color, fancy shapes, push buttons, and so on, all cost more, not once, but every month thereafter; they are not necessary. Second extensions may be useful in big or busy houses and are not expensive; but other extras *are* expensive and hardly worth the cost for most people.

You will be charged a basic monthly rate which includes a fixed number of local calls. Calls beyond that number or for longer distances will be added to the monthly bill. You can send telegrams and cables from your home telephone; these too will appear on your telephone bill at the end of the month.

When your telephone is installed, you will be given two directories—the local one, which is alphabetical, and the Classified Directory (often called "The Yellow Pages" for obvious reasons). It is worthwhile to sit down and really study both these books when you first get them. They contain a great deal of information about using the telephone, special services that are available (including time, weather, or traffic information), rates, times of the week when one can phone most cheaply, and so on. The "Classified" lists all businesses, organizations, restaurants, stores, and services in your area in such a way that you can quickly find whatever you need. If you study that directory, you will learn much about your city and the range of what is available; for example: the schools, clubs, organizations, public swimming pools; all kinds of instruction and classes; where to buy special foods or spices; where to have repairs made on all sorts of goods; restaurants by nationality; places where you can *rent* television sets, records, children's cribs, crutches, fur coats or a wide range of articles (look under "Rental Service").

The Classified Directory, which is corrected and updated every year, can become one of your best friends if you take the trouble to get to know it well.

Telephone Credit Cards

As soon as you have your own telephone—and therefore your own number—you can call the Business Office of the Telephone Company and ask for a Credit Card. This is free and a great convenience. It enables you to make calls or send cables from any telephone, public or private, and have the call charged to your home account. This often saves you from having to struggle with exact change in a telephone booth or makes it possible to call from a friend's home or office without imposing on his generosity.

Public Telephones

Different countries put their public telephones in different places! Here they are widespread. You will find them in bus and air terminals, railroad stations, stores, hotels, the lobbies of many office buildings, restaurants, gasoline stations, and in small booths along streets and highways. Instructions for use are found on each phone. You will need a dime (10 cents) to reach the operator or to make a local call. Long-distance and overseas calls can also be made from public telephones, but they require a handful of change in nickels, dimes, and quarters. If you would like the recipient to pay the charges, ask the operator to make it a "Collect" call. You can ask the operator what the charges will be for a three-minute call before you place it; if you ask her to do so, she will tell you when your three minutes are up. You can talk longer, but must pay another charge.

Two Types of Long-Distance Calls

One can make calls either "person-to-person" or "station-to-station." "Person-to-person" is far more expensive, but you only pay charges from the time you actually begin speaking to the person you ask for. If you are uncertain of his/her being there and are calling from a long distance, this is worthwhile. In "station-to-station" calls, you start to pay from the moment the call goes through, no matter who answers. This is the better method, for it is much cheaper, if you think your person is likely to be there or if you merely want to leave a message.

TELEGRAMS AND CABLES

The Western Union Company handles telegrams and cables in the United States and overseas, but they are not recommended for fast, reliable service. It is better to *telephone* anything urgent in the States or to use I.T.T. (International Telephone and Telegraph) or R.C.A. for cables abroad. Both R.C.A. and I.T.T. offer Full Rate Telegrams (called FR), which are the fastest; Letter Telegrams (LT), which is an overnight service; and Telex Transmission, which is charged by the minute, not by the word, and is useful to those who send a volume of international telegrams. Look up either company in the phone book or send your message through Western Union with the words "Via ITT" or "Via RCA" after the address.

None of these are sent from the post office as they are in many other countries. You send them via telephone. If you must send a cable from a pay telephone, ask the operator the charges in advance so you can be sure to have the correct change. A credit card is a blessing in such a case. Rates are based on the number of words. The names and addresses of persons sending and receiving the message are not counted as part of the message within the United States, but in cables or radiograms going overseas, they are.

There are various types of local messages:

The "straight" telegram:

This is the quickest but most expensive; it allows 15 words for the minimum charge.

The Night Letter:

This is the least expensive, but slowest, being held for delivery until the following morning.

The Day Letter:

This falls between the two, taking longer than a straight telegram but being delivered during the same day. This allows 50 words (rather than 15) for its minimum charge.

"HAM" (OR AMATEUR) RADIO

If you are concerned about family or friends at home or want to celebrate some special festival, it is worth investigating the possibilities of communicating by means of an amateur or "ham" radio operator. There are thousands of them scattered throughout the world, chatting with one another across the miles. They are often delighted to transmit a friendly message or to put you "on the air" to talk directly for a minute or two. You cannot use these wavelengths for business, but if you simply want to hear the voice of a friend or relative, it can be arranged.

The first step is to find an amateur radio operator. Often the engineers at one of the local radio or television stations are amateur operators in their free time, or they know someone who is; any substantial radio store is likely to know the local "hams" who buy equipment from them. Sometimes you can spot a "ham" by the enormous antenna mounted on his car. Often if you ask around among the people you meet, someone will recommend a friend who enjoys the hobby.

Once you locate an operator, he will inform you of the next steps. They have their own worldwide directories listing the call letters of all other "hams." He will find the person located nearest your friend and will arrange with him to make an appointment with your friend so that you can talk together over the airwaves. You cannot abuse the privilege—you are asking people for favors and are not licensed to communicate—but for a brief contact on a special occasion or in case of an emergency, it is possible.

Chapter 13

Safety and Emergencies

Everyone knows that cities grow ever more violent and full of trouble; however, one need not "live scared." If one follows certain normal procedures, minds one's own business, and stays away from dark, unsavory places, the chances of having a misfortune—while not totally removed—are very much diminished.

ON THE STREETS

Keep to the more traveled and better-lit streets after dark; if you have to move through "bad" areas, go by bus or taxi. Try to board your bus in a populated area so you do not have to wait at a bus stop in a lonely locality.

Avoid parks after dark; walk on the nonpark side if you are passing a park. Much of today's violence in the United States is taking place because drug-users are desperate for money for a "fix." Such people loiter in dark places waiting to hold up defenseless persons and take their money; they like the edges of parks because they can make a quick escape.

Railroad and bus stations are often loitering places for unsavory people at night. If you have to wait in a terminal during evening or night hours, do so in the main waiting room where it is light and people are passing, or else choose a place within sight of a guard or policeman.

Avoid subway travel after 9 P.M. at night if you can and also on weekends when subways—with their subterranean tunnels—are likely to be fairly deserted.

SECURITY AT HOME

Locks only work if you use them! Never leave the door to your apartment unlocked; be careful not to leave a key in the door by mistake even for a short while; don't leave your door open, ajar, or unlocked even if you are just going out to empty the trash or talk with a neighbor.

Especially at night, it is a good precaution to keep the inside chain on the door. Most city apartments have "peepholes" through which you can see who is at your door before you open it; others have TV systems in the front lobby or some voice identification arrangement. USE WHATEVER SYSTEM IS PROVIDED. It is there for your protection. DON'T OPEN A DOOR UNTIL YOU KNOW WHO IS THERE. Don't admit a salesman, a repairman, or a delivery boy unless you have ordered from them or are expecting them. Be *sure* of who is at your door before you open it.

If you live near the ground floor or facing a fire escape and are worried about your windows, talk to the superintendent about window locks or extra metal screens.

None of this is meant to frighten you, but it is just common sense. If you use the various safeguards that exist, then you can feel secure, relaxed, and protected. If you do not, you are taking a chance nowadays in any major city of the world.

Should you lock yourself out of your apartment by mistake, the superintendent can let you in again. He will have a master key for such emergencies. Some people also leave a spare key with a trusted neighbor for just such moments of need.

It is nice to know that in most large cities there are locksmiths available on 24-hour duty. Look under "Locksmiths" in the Classified Directory. Such a man can be a lifesaver if, for example, you break off the key in your car lock after a party some night!!

FIRE

Follow the trash instructions for your apartment house; do no burning of trash on your own.

Never leave the apartment—even for a minute—while anything is cooking, especially in oil.

If a fire *does* break out, call the building superintendent, doorman, or elevator operator *immediately,* however small it is. Dial "0" for operator on the telephone and tell her *where the fire is.*

Most apartment fires are caused by burning fat or by an electric wire or by a cigarette. All homes should have a small foam fire extinguisher near the stove; these are good for either fat or electrical fires. You can buy small ones for under $10 at any hardware shop, and should do so. *Be sure to check the date on it before you buy—* they deteriorate with age. Baking soda is good to smother flames quickly.

INSURANCE

You might think this subject need not concern you. Unfortunately, however, there is a growing need for everyone to carry liability insurance because an increasing number of people are claiming high damages after even the simplest and most ordinary of accidents. This may be another sad result of the drug scene or growing unemployment or the various turmoils of our time. If someone trips on your front step, or your dog knocks over a child, or your cleaning woman gets burned on your stove, they could—and a growing number do—enter a lawsuit against you and claim damages out of all proportion. Courts assume that one is covered by insurance, and so they often award far more in "damages" than would seem reasonable to most of us. If you do *not* carry insurance for such a situation, you can be in bad financial trouble.

The term to inquire about is "comprehensive liability." An insur-

ance agent will advise you about the proper level of coverage for
your income, the size of your family, and so on. Talk to him freely.
Be sure to consult a responsible man who will not "oversell" you
beyond your needs. You should find him through your firm or
someone you know in a bank, or a friend, or a lawyer. When you
get the agent's advice, it is a good idea to "double-check" by discussing his recommendations with a colleague in your office before
actually signing any contract. Never let the agent rush you; the
more he tries to, the more cautious you should be.

You should also seek advice on other kinds of insurance according to the value of your possessions and property. If you have not
brought over any jewelry, fine paintings, or furniture, you may not
need to carry such property insurance as fire or theft, but you
should discuss this carefully with a knowledgeable person who can
judge in relation to your belongings. Insurance is expensive; one
can easily be talked into "overinsuring" goods that could be replaced without too much trouble if they were lost. You will never
receive the full value from your insurance anyway; often it works
out to be a very small percentage of the value. The fine print on the
contract is confusing, but extremely important. Do get someone
who understands contracts to go over yours with you in detail.

Generally speaking, you need cover only a few selected, expensive, and irreplaceable material possessions (such as jewels, furs, or
cameras, for example) for theft, but in addition: you need to be
well covered against liability, in case of being sued; you need adequate health and accident insurance because medical costs are so
high here (see Chapter 10); and you need substantial auto insurance if you plan to drive (see Chapter 8).

Part II

FOR THOSE WHO STAY LONGER

Chapter 14

Housing

HOW TO BEGIN LOOKING

As is true in cities throughout the world, the farther out from any urban center, generally the lower the rents will be. However, transportation is so overcrowded and expensive that one has to balance these two factors in deciding where to settle. Naturally it is easier to take part in the life of a city if one is close to the center. For this reason single people or childless couples usually prefer not to live too far out. However, families with children generally tend to settle in the suburbs. They do so in search of larger houses at lower rents, less crowded schools, and a slower pace—not to mention grass and trees!

If your children are of school age, the quality of local schools should be of primary concern *before you decide on any home.* Many families have found that in the end it was cheaper to move to a fairly expensive suburb which had good public schools rather than a cheaper neighborhood where inadequate or crowded public schools forced them to send their children to costly private schools. If there are many children in a family, this is particularly important to consider.

Once the school question has been looked into, commuting conditions for the husband should be investigated. Some directions out from each city are likely to be easier than others—better train or bus schedules, less crowded routes, more alternatives, shorter trips, and so on.

Your employer should be able to give you helpful advice about schools and commuter schedules in various areas that surround the city. You will be able to judge a good deal for yourself by driving through a number of neighborhoods. Stop and chat with people you see outside their houses; talk to the librarian or the man who runs the drugstore or the village market; investigate and "feel out" a neighborhood if you possibly can before you actually select one. Towns vary greatly even when situated next to one another.

SOURCES OF INFORMATION

Your best source of information about either houses or apartments is likely to be the local paper. As a rule the week's most complete real estate section appears in the Sunday edition. Try to get a copy on *Saturday!* Usually the real estate section is printed early; the local newsstand may be able to sell you one even if you have to stay up late into the evening to buy it. Time is important as there is often tremendous competition for housing. You need to do your combing of the columns the night before so that on Sunday morning you can telephone early to any likely looking prospects. You can start telephoning as early as 7 A.M.

There are real estate agents in all localities. These can be helpful, but if you can find a house yourself through friends or the newspaper or by seeing a "For Rent" sign, it is far better. Agents charge steep fees—a month's rent is common, sometimes 10 percent of the year's rent. Some companies pay such fees for their employees; others do not. Be certain you understand your company's policy regarding this matter, or else inquire about fees before you sign with any real estate agency.

IF YOU RENT A HOUSE

In addition to the rent, you will generally be expected to pay for gas and electricity, heat and hot water, and simple electrical and plumbing repairs.

You also provide and pay for normal maintenance such as grass-cutting, window-washing, leaf-raking, and snow removal. If the house has a sidewalk, you (not the town) are responsible for having it clear of snow within a few hours after each snowfall (usually four daylight hours).

FURNISHED APARTMENTS OR HOUSES

The word "furnished" means different things to different people. You will normally be supplied with the essentials: stove, refrigerator, beds, chairs, sofa, tables, lamps, minimal china and glass, flatware (often rather poor), basic kitchen supplies, curtains, some pictures; sometimes, but not always, a small supply of bed, bath, and table linens. There will be some—but usually not enough—blankets.

You will need to supply: your favorite kitchen utensils, some table linens or mats, extra lamps, coat hangers, whatever electrical appliances you want—such as toasters, irons, etc.; usually also extra bed linens and blankets. You certainly will want to bring enough of your own things to make you feel familiar and comfortable. Your own pictures, books, sofa cushions, and the like will make it seem more like "home" to you.

TO BRING OR NOT TO BRING?

When you realize how expensive it is to ship household goods, you will agree that it often makes better sense to buy basic equipment here such as dishes, sheets, towels, saucepans, etc., rather than to ship your own unless, of course, your company is assuming all shipping costs.

Furthermore, you may want to think carefully about bringing any pieces you cherish such as that delicate clock, grandfather's Chippendale desk, your prized elephant tusk chair. The best rule to follow is: *If the item were lost or broken, would you grieve? Or could you accept the insurance money and not care too deeply?*

Picture for yourself the crate being lifted by a ship's crane and then dropped into the ship's hold or riding out a monsoon on a dock. Probably neither of these things will happen to your things; most goods today are packed to survive, but think about such hazards. You may decide to leave home your most valued possessions!

One more guideline: What will the climate be like in that part of the United States to which you are going? If you will be in sunny California, hot Arizona, or moist Florida, you should consider leaving heavy rugs, big upholstered chairs, velvet draperies, and the like at home. In hot areas most people use rattan, glass, wicker, and so on; they leave most of their floors uncovered and use louvers or shutters rather than draperies at the windows.

WHAT DO THE RENTAL WORDS MEAN?

Even "native" Americans are confused by the terms used in real estate advertisements. A tiny hallway, an alcove off the kitchen, or an "L" in the living room may be called a "room." Sometimes kitchens and bathrooms are counted as rooms, and sometimes they are not. When you see "$2\frac{1}{2}$ rooms" listed, you cannot be certain what this means. Neither can Americans! The only safe thing to do is to ask in each case: "Exactly what rooms are included in this apartment?" Ask to see a floor plan if you can; ask the sizes of the rooms. Floor plans can make a place look larger than in fact it is— and far more glamorous! Apartments are more expensive as you go higher in a building. You are paying for more light and less dirt and noise from the street.

HOUSING AGREEMENTS

Don't sign any agreement until you have consulted a member of your company's personnel department, or a lawyer, or a real estate man at your bank or a well-recommended real estate agent.

You should understand clearly *in advance* what the lease says about: ending the lease; renewing it if you want to stay longer; pro-

visions for damages; number of occupants; rules about children or
pets; whether or not you can sublet; when the next price rise will
occur and what it is likely to be; painting or redecoration regulations; hidden charges—sometimes extra ones suddenly appear for
such items as a TV aerial, garbage removal, or a fee for a night
watchman.

Rents are payable one month in advance, on the first day of each
month. When you lease an apartment, you are normally asked for
one month's "security deposit" in addition to the first month's rent.
This will be returned to you when you leave if there has been no
major damage to the premises during your occupancy. The landlord or his agent will do the inspecting. This is not the last month's
rent; it is an assurance to the landlord that if you damage the
premises he will be covered. For your own protection, you should
examine the apartment carefully *before* you sign a lease and get the
landlord's or his agent's signed (written) acknowledgment for any
breaks, cracks, stains, or other damages that existed before you be-
came the tenant. Otherwise you may be charged with these two or
three years later when you leave.

If you should be transferred before your lease runs out, you will
have to negotiate with the landlord to end your responsibility unless this provision is already written into your original lease.

You may have to pay the rent until he can find another tenant.

All such matters should be discussed in advance. Be *sure* to get
professional legal advice before signing your name to anything.
Once a contract is signed, it becomes binding. It cannot be canceled and the terms cannot be changed without the greatest legal
difficulty. Furthermore, you will then have no leeway for any further negotiations.

And so, to summarize, before you sign:

1. Be sure you know which services and utilities are or are not
included in the rent—electricity, gas, air conditioning, TV antenna,
washing machine, etc.

2. Determine whether or not you have to pay a brokerage fee (if

you found the apartment through an agent). If so, how much will it be?

3. How often will the landlord repaint the apartment? Will he pay for the painting or will you?

4. Exactly how long does the lease run? (They vary.)

5. What are the conditions under which you can end the lease if you should be transferred?

6. If you should want to sublet to someone else, can you? Under what conditions?

7. Does the landlord know the size of your family? Not all apartment houses allow children. Does this one?

8. Not all apartment houses allow pets. Have *written* permission if you are going to keep a pet.

UTILITIES—GAS, ELECTRICITY, HEAT, AIR CONDITIONING, AND WATER

In most large cities stoves burn what is called "city gas"; in country areas bottled gas is often used for stoves. Some housewives prefer electric stoves, even though they are slower to heat, because the heat is considered more even.

Most U.S. heating systems today are oil burners operated by electric motors or else coal furnaces.

Modern apartment buildings are nearly always equipped with centrally operated air conditioning which can be adjusted by the occupants of each apartment. If you live in an older house, it is likely to have window air conditioners; if there are no window units and the need is great, one can rent air conditioners on a monthly basis for the few hot months.

Normally fees for gas and electricity are *not* included in the monthly rent. Both bills will come from the electric company, but the gas bill will be itemized separately.

Most of the country has 110–120 volt current, 60 cycles, A.C. A few older houses and areas are still wired for D.C. Unless your own small appliances are geared for U.S. current or have been converted, you are well advised to leave them home. For small items, transformers can be a nuisance, although they work well for major appliances such as refrigerators or stoves. However, you can buy all kinds of appliances here at reasonable prices.

In most cities there is no charge for water, but outside city limits it may be metered, in which case you pay either monthly or quarterly. Water rates are low.

You can drink water safely from taps anywhere in the United States. Do NOT drink from brooks, wells, streams, or rivers, however. Pollution is, alas, widespread.

Tap water may taste unpleasant because it contains a high percentage of purifying chemicals. If you find this obnoxious, you can buy bottled water in the supermarket.

MOVING YOUR BELONGINGS

If you are going into a furnished apartment or house, moving is a relatively simple matter. You move exactly as you would for a stay in a hotel, though you might bring a few extra items as indicated above.

If you are moving all your household goods to this country, you or your company will probably have arranged the transfer through a specialist. Large national and international movers have experienced packers and good equipment. You should "inventory" all your belongings carefully, making separate lists of 1) those items which are going into storage, 2) those going to your new home, and 3) those going to be given away or cared for in some other way. (There is always this third category!)

Inventories should be reasonably detailed, but you can group together such items as:

kitchen utensils—x number of boxes;
children's clothing—x number of boxes;
contents of desk—x number of boxes, etc.

You do not have to itemize down to the last spoon!

This is crucial advice: Have the items which you are leaving in storage picked up on an earlier day than the rest of your inventory. Many people have the whole job done on the same day, mistakenly thinking that this is easier. It is *not!* More than one family will tell a horrendous story of having arrived at their final destination and waited weeks for their furnishings only to discover that, through some unaccountable error, the movers had confused the loads. Facing them were the goods for storage while all that they really needed was now left far behind!

Before any packers come, you should sort out the two categories into separate groupings as much as you can. Mark storage goods with a colored tag or sticker to make the difference as visible as possible. Then still carefully supervise the movers as they work.

As the boxes are being packed for your new destination, mark each completed carton clearly in large letters on the outside: "books"—"children's toys"—"kitchen supplies." This will help both the movers and you when you finally get into your new home.

When your belongings do arrive, you must be present to receive the goods. As the movers unpack, check to see that each item has arrived in good condition. The man in charge of the moving crew should make a written note of any damage *before you sign the bill.* Once you sign it, he will make no further changes. If some goods are damaged, immediately obtain a claim form from the moving company (or their insurance agent). Fill it out, *have a Xerox copy made of it for yourself,* then return the original promptly. Time is important. Don't delay. Let your own company know what has happened too so that their transportation specialist can advise you. If you are not reimbursed within two or three weeks, let the transportation officer of your firm follow-up on your claim, or do it yourself. Don't let too much time go by.

Photocopies should always be made of whatever papers or letters or claims or counterclaims pass between you and the movers and/or the insurance company. This is very important. If your company does not make the copies for you, take each paper to a public copying machine. You will find them in stationers' shops, libraries, railroad stations, and even Woolworth stores! They are simple to operate and cost only a few cents.

Having the full story in detail and in the proper sequence in your files makes following up on any claim far easier and quicker.

At no stage in the moving process should you yourself touch *anything* once the movers have arrived. Let them do *all* the packing and moving, with no exceptions. This is very important because otherwise you may cancel out all their insurance coverage. If you have touched *nothing*, then nothing can be your fault. Otherwise, everything can!

It is well to check carefully with your company some days before the movers are to arrive so that you know exactly what services you can expect. These vary according to the contract. Some will place your furniture, set up beds, and unpack china, silver, glassware, linens, and books. They are supposed to remove all packing debris. Some movers will connect your electrical appliances for you; most will not. Some will only set up large items and will not unpack small ones. Arrangements vary widely so you need to find out ahead of time which ones will apply to you. Be sure to *ask* in advance.

It is not necessary to tip the moving crew, but most people do so in relation to the size and length of the job. Tips range from $1 a man for a small job up to about $5 per man for a full day's job. It is also a good idea to have beer and coffee available if possible. This is a hard and tiring job. Be friendly with the movers, but try to stay out of their way. Time is money for them and also for you.

Chapter 15

The Most for Your Money

One newcomer to the United States, when asked his first impression, replied: "So many things to buy." And so there are!

MATERIALISM

You will find yourself being urged from every page of every newspaper and on every TV wavelength to buy all manner of goods which, in fact, you are quite happy without! This constant barrage of advertising, with its emphasis on owning this or that in order to be happy, healthy, or "more attractive," has given America the reputation of being dreadfully materialistic. It is true; this is an affluent and, therefore, materialistic nation. But it is interesting to note that as soon as *any* country grows in affluence, its "materialism" also becomes apparent. Traffic jams develop in country after country as more people are able to buy cars; salesmen work harder and harder in most of the free world to sell televisions, watches, new furniture, new foods, new clothes, transistor radios, or labor-saving machines such as computers, tractors, or washing machines.

One must assume that humans everywhere are alike in this respect. As soon as there is any extra money, they seek to raise and *keep on raising* their family's standard of living. One need not be shocked at this, but should look at the deeper level: What do people then do with their new leisure? How much do they share it? How creative are they? How hard do they work?

Because most things in the United States are mass-produced, there is greatly increased leisure. You will find there is also a tremendous range in prices, variation often being based on quality rather than style, but also on other factors. This can be misleading to a newcomer. An eighteen-year-old stenographer on her first job can afford snappy-looking clothes, a TV, a shared apartment, a winter cruise (on the installment plan). This is startling to those who come from countries where such luxuries are attainable only by the ultra-rich. This girl pays less and gets shoddier goods than her older colleague who can afford better quality—but the quick effect on the onlooker has been made, and the girl herself feels sophisticated. Almost surely she will shift upward in quality as she both earns and learns more. This is how our mobile social structure works.

From all of America's abundance, how are you, the new arrival, going to know how to get your money's worth? In the first place, don't hurry. Take time; look over the various kinds of stores and examine the quality of their merchandise; read the ads carefully so that you can compare prices; touch, explore, and examine before you buy.

In addition, there are some helpful guidelines.

FOOD

Supermarkets in someone else's country are always confusing. How can you decide what to buy amid such profusion?

Grades and Prices

You can save a good deal of money if you buy according to *grade* instead of "brand" (which only means company name).

For example, one can of beans may cost 31 cents; another, 26 cents. The more expensive one may be the *brand* that is most widely advertised and therefore best known; perhaps you are only paying your share of the advertising costs. It is quite possible that if you buy the cheaper can, you will *not* be sacrificing quality, yet you will save several cents on just one small item.

Look to see if both cans contain the same number of ounces;

look at the list of ingredients to see what percentage is water. By actual law ingredients must always be listed. The important thing to know is that the listing must be *in the order of the amount contained.* So if the ingredients read: "water, macaroni, cheese," you put the package back on the shelf for you know it contains more water than macaroni.

Watch out for such words as "moisture"—which means nothing more nor less than "water"—or "salad dressing" as distinct from "mayonnaise." The law says that mayonnaise must contain 65 percent oil. So some companies put out "salad dressing," which only has to contain 30 percent oil. Some people prefer less oil, but it is good to know what you are getting so you can judge the price accordingly.

The thing that is confusing but important to understand is that our grading system (the words "Choice" or "Good" on meat, for example, or "Grade A" or "Grade B" on eggs) has *nothing* to do with the *nutritional* value of the food. All will be fresh, healthy, and nutritious. The difference in grade has to do only with *appearance*— more uniform size, whole and not in pieces, better color, less water. Let us take canned mushrooms as an example: Grades (and therefore prices) will vary depending on whether the mushrooms are whole, sliced, or in broken pieces. But *all will be good, healthy mushrooms.*

Or tomatoes: Do you need firm, uniform-sized tomatoes for a salad, for instance (Grade A), or are you going to serve them in a stew or sauce? If so, broken pieces of various sizes would be perfectly all right for your purpose (Grades B or C).

In short, when speaking of canned goods:

Grade A—Means whole, beautiful, free from defects;
Grade B—Means large pieces, but not necessarily whole;
Grade C—Means smaller and broken pieces, often lots of juice; satisfactory for cooking, but not for appearance.

The price of Grade C may be half the price of Grade A!

Much citizen pressure is being put on the U.S. government to regulate and grade foods. As yet the grading system is not compulsory, so one does not find grades on everything. However, the U.S. Department of Agriculture is marking more and more items. It is a good idea to look for their stamp and use it whenever possible.

For example: one market offered three brands of orange juice. Prices were: 47 cents, 49 cents, and 53 cents. All three brands had a small shield printed on the can with the words "U.S. Grade A"; all three contained the same number of ounces. This meant that all three brands met the same government standards of quality. The difference in price therefore was a matter of packaging, advertising, or transportation costs. It was *not* the quality of the juice. So you can save by learning to read labels.

This same sort of price variation appears also on cigarettes, camera film, and many other common items. If in doubt, ask your friends, neighbors, and colleagues for their recommendations. (See Appendix, Part II for a list of government food grades and symbols.)

Warnings

Although an increasing effort is being made to protect the buyer, there are still, unfortunately, a number of "shortcuts" or "hidden" factors that one needs to watch out for.

Sizes and weights, for example. A bottle that looks like a quart (or liter) does not necessarily contain that amount. In tiny print on the label, it may say "Contains 24 fluid ounces." (A quart is 32.) Packages meant to look like one pound may actually contain only 14 or 11 or 9 ounces worth of food. By law, weights are printed on all food packages, under "Net Contents," so one can always look and see—but too many of us do not take the time and trouble. Often the print is very small—on purpose!

Don't be overly concerned about all these matters; you will gradually learn by experience and by trial and error, but you can shorten your learning time if you read labels and compare as you shop. You will soon find the foods your family likes and will learn which brands are best for you. Such care and study can save you a considerable amount on your food bills. The Department of Agriculture says that those who watch carefully and who follow the "weekly specials" offered in all supermarkets can save in the neighborhood of 6 percent per week.

CLOTHES AND FABRICS

To judge the weave, quality, weight, and texture of cloth, each person has to feel it and decide for herself. But labels are sewn into clothes too to help you know the content of the fabric—if you stop to read them!

Suppose you buy a blouse advertised as a Dacron (drip-dry) blouse. How do you know what it is really made of? By law it *must* have a label attached telling the percentage of every kind of fiber used in the material.

Perhaps the label says: "cotton 30%, rayon 30%, Dacron 40%"; perhaps it will say "100% Dacron"; or it might include only 8% Dacron. But it could still be advertised as a "Dacron blouse."

Many people never look at labels, but if you do, you will know what you are actually getting—which might make a difference as to whether or not you want to buy it at a given price.

Buying Woolen Goods

The law states that the label must tell how much is new wool— which is called simply "wool"; how much is reused or reprocessed wool; and how much is other fibers—such as cotton or rayon.

Generally speaking, the more new wool, the better—but not always. You must feel it and judge for yourself. Sometimes a mixture of good quality new wool (at least *half*) might be better than a 100 percent wool garment, if the quality of new wool was poor in the first place.

RETURNING MERCHANDISE

If you have bought something and want to return it, you can do so with most items from nearly all department stores and often—but not always—from smaller shops. However, you must follow two rules or they will not accept the returned item:

1) The return must be made *within 10 days* of purchase;
2) You *must* have the sales slip with it.

So do not throw away any receipts, however thin and skimpy they may look, until you are sure you are satisfied with the item.

If you are returning a gift and therefore have no sales receipt, take off the delivery label from the front of the package. It has various little notes and marks on it that have meaning for the clerk. If you have no label, then ask to "exchange" for some item of equal worth. It is often easier to do this than to get a cash refund.

GUARANTEES

When you buy new electric appliances, radios, TV's, or other major items such as stoves, you will probably be given a sheaf of papers with them. One of these is likely to be a written guarantee. This means that if anything goes wrong, you can have the item repaired free of charge for a certain length of time—on some items as long as three to five years. You should read the guarantee carefully. It probably asks you to send in a postcard to establish the date of purchase. If so, be *sure* to do it. In addition, write the date of purchase on the guarantee itself along with the guarantee number. Keep it somewhere safe so you can find it if you need it. The guarantee will be of help *only* if you have saved the papers and complied with the instructions.

REPAIRS

If you have problems with vacuum cleaners, toasters, radios, and so on, look under "Electric Appliances—Repairs" or "Radio (Vacuum cleaner, etc.) Repair" in the classified section of the telephone book. Try to find a repair shop specializing in your particular brand name, if possible. Other kinds of repairs—china, glass, zippers, etc.—are also listed by item in most phone books.

Telephone Sales

If anyone tries to sell you an item over the telephone, just say "No, thank you" and hang up without any further conversation. Dancing lessons, stocks, light bulbs, magazines—all sorts of things may be offered. *Don't get involved!* They will try to tempt you with every kind of prize, free demonstration, or gift. *Don't fall for it.* Reputable firms rarely use this technique for selling—any more than they use door-to-door salesmen. Newcomers to the United States should take *no chances* with telephone salesmen. It is dangerous to do so.

INSTALLMENT PLANS

Generally speaking, *avoid* installment plan buying. Costs of carrying and amortization are high and often so confusing that they are virtually hidden. Once you have signed the agreement, you are stuck with all the payments; there is no way out. So tread carefully. Mortgages on real estate, well-handled financing on the price of a car, or similar loans on very large purchases may be necessary, but try to avoid burdening yourself with monthly payments on such luxury items as washers, TV's, hi-fi's, or tempting trips to sunny beaches in the Caribbean! You often pay one third or one half as much again as the regular price by the time all fees have been figured.

BUYING WHERE IT COSTS LESS

Americans do not usually "bargain" over prices, as is familiar in much of the world. What they do instead is shop around to find the store which offers the item and quality they want at the lowest price. Almost everything sold in the United States varies in price according to the store and often the time of year (just before Christmas is highest; lowest is just after Christmas or during mid-August sales). Sometimes the price varies according to state or local taxes. Many people cross state lines to buy liquor, cigarettes, or automobiles, for example, because there are wide variations in taxes on such items from state to state.

Discount Houses

If it is important to you to save money, look for the discount houses in your city. They exist all across the country and are of course growing in popularity in these days of inflation. Much of what they sell is comparable to goods sold elsewhere, but they can offer lower prices for various reasons or a combination of them: perhaps the store offers no credit terms—therefore it saves on that operation; it may remain open for longer hours; there may be fewer sales people and less service; usually there is no delivery service except for heavy items like refrigerators; floor space is often so fully used that the store is congested; the decor is simple or non-existent so as to save the cost of fancy carpeting or expensive interiors; dressing rooms, where you try clothes on, may be communal.

In most discount houses you will find clothes hanging on long racks; shoes may even be piled up in "bins." Your best buys in these places are apt to be such standard "name" items as: drugs and cosmetics, photographic equipment, housewares, bedding, small appliances, garden equipment, carpets and rugs, luggage, books and records, furniture or large household appliances, rather than clothing.

Many of these are the very same items that you would buy in other stores at higher prices. Never look in discount stores for top-quality clothes or exclusive fashions or choice furniture. Look for goods where serviceability is more important than style (pots and pans, blue jeans, garden hoses, and so on).

Another popular American institution is the so-called dime store. No longer selling much for a dime, these stores originated in the nineteenth century when Mr. Woolworth decided that a small profit on a great volume would add up to more than a large profit on fewer sales. So he opened a chain of stores selling an enormous range of items for (in those days) 5¢ and 10¢—nothing higher. These prices have long since gone, but the various chains which have followed Woolworth's (Grant's, Kresge's, Lamston's, Murphy's, Green's) still carry an extraordinary variety of inexpensive items. Because they are so colorful and give such a good idea of what is available, these various "Five and Ten" stores are often of interest to newcomers who find that wandering through them also helps them to learn American names for unfamiliar items.

Buying Secondhand

So many people are constantly on the move in the United States that it is easy to find secondhand household goods for sale. Buying secondhand is quite usual here. Many young couples furnish new homes this way or people who do not want to spend time shopping sometimes buy the entire contents of an apartment from someone who is moving to another part of the country.

If you look in the local newspaper, you will see advertisements in the classified section that read:

"Moving; entire contents of house for sale."
"Going to California; have desk, large clock, child's bicycle for sale."

"Redecorated house; complete living room furniture for sale—
Louis XIV style."

If you see something that interests you, call *at once* on the telephone; such things are often sold very quickly. If it is still available,
go immediately to examine it. If you like an item, you can try bar-
gaining. Then you must work out a means of getting the goods to
your house. This can be a major problem, but the easiest solution
(if you have no friend with a car) is to look again at ads in the local
paper or in the Classified Directory under "Trucking" to find a
man with a truck. Prices range from about $5 to about $15 an hour,
depending on the locality. Give a deposit to hold the goods and *get
a receipt.* Don't pay the full price until you come back with the
truck to pick up the items. Most people are honest and are dealing
in a straightforward manner, but there can be "rackets"—so you
need to be a little wary.

Buying in this way is a good deal more trouble than buying new
equipment and having it delivered, but it can also be much
cheaper. Many times, you get real bargains and very high quality,
especially if the owner must move and is in a hurry to dispose of his
goods or if someone has died and an estate is being settled.

Thrift Shops

Thrift shops are run by charities which first collect and then sell
used clothes, bric-a-brac, sports equipment, books, china, glassware, and so on. The charities then donate the monies they collect
to some particular school, hospital, old people's home, or other institution.

There is no "loss of face" in buying at such shops. Many of the
wealthiest "Jet Set" society people donate to them, help to run
them, and also buy from them. They are particularly good for such
items as children's clothes (often outgrown before they were much
used) or evening dresses which the well-to-do "donate" after a few

wearings, but which most of us wear so seldom that we want to buy at minimum cost! Many people go to thrift shops for fur coats, ice skates, tennis rackets, books, or for pictures, lamps, or "extras" of that sort for their new homes. By law all clothing given to reputable shops has been dry-cleaned and inspected so you need have no worries about that if you select a well-run charity shop.

Chapter 16

Household Help and Baby-Sitters

Domestic help is so expensive nowadays that most Americans do their own housework. The only common exceptions are:

1) Cleaning women who come in once or twice a week;
2) Baby-sitters who stay with children when the parents go out.

For the rest, precooked and packaged foods, disposable or no-iron fabrics, dishwashers and washing machines, laundromats and coin-operated dry cleaners—all such time- and labor-saving devices—take the place of household help.

TO FIND A CLEANING WOMAN

The best way is by word of mouth. Start with your friends or the wives of your husband's business acquaintances. This is a normal request, and you need not feel embarrassed. Americans are accustomed to helping each other find domestic help as it is difficult to do so. People will ask their own help if they have extra time to give, or a niece or a friend to suggest.

Ask the superintendent of your apartment house. Perhaps there is someone already working in the building who has extra time. This will *not* be the superintendent's daughter or sister, as would be true in much of the world, but he often knows the tenants' "help" and can ask them. If he finds someone for you, he will expect a tip —$5 or up depending on circumstances. Sometimes the clerks at local laundries, groceries, or the like can give you suggestions. If you are known to be a regular customer, such people are likely to recommend carefully.

If you cannot find anyone by word of mouth, there are other methods—though these tend to be less satisfactory:

You can use a Maid Service (listed as such in the Classified Directory).

Such services are expensive, but on the other hand they look after troublesome details like Social Security payments, insurance, and so on. There are House Cleaning Services, too. They send a team of well-equipped men in to wash windows, clean rugs, and do similar heavy work at regular intervals—or once or twice a year as you request.

You can use an Employment Agency.

This is likely to be expensive and is not a preferred way. There is no guarantee that the person will stay with you beyond the period covered by the usually high agency fee.

Furthermore, you may have to interview many people. If you use this method, be *sure* to ask for references and be *sure* to consult a good agency. They vary widely.

You can advertise.

Also not a good way, as you know nothing about the people who may come streaming into your house to be interviewed. If you do follow this method, check each reference very carefully before hiring. Don't try it unless your English is good.

You can answer an advertisement.

People in small towns or country areas can answer local ads and usually find help; if you are in a larger town, it is also a possible method if you interview carefully and check references. Some of the best prospects are found in foreign language papers.

IF YOU NEED HELP FOR A PARTY

If you have a cleaning woman and find her efficient, you can ask if she would like to help you serve in the evening; often they are willing. Sometimes they have friends whom they recommend, or they may send their daughters.

If you would rather have trained help, look under "Maid Service" in the trusty Classified Directory. You can hire waitresses, cooks, bartenders, or butlers by the hour.

If you live in a college town, call the Employment Bureau of the university. Some colleges hold extracurricular training programs in household skills or bartending to help students in getting jobs; other students just sign up for general help and can be hired by the hour. Some are excellent helpers; others are sloppy and irresponsible. Try to interview before your party so you can judge for yourself.

BABY-SITTERS

Today only one person in five in the United States lives within 50 miles of his birthplace. Since the country was first settled, Americans have moved around a great deal, and are often far away from their parents. Because they have broken ties with their past at quite young ages, chosen their own occupations, established their own homes, and developed their own lifestyles, few American children grow up closely surrounded by grandparents, aunts, uncles, and cousins as they do in Italy, Nigeria, or India, for example. This, along with the fact that modern American families do not have servants, has made the "baby-sitter" a vital part of the American scene. A "sitter" is someone who is hired to care for children for a specific length of time—usually relatively short—while the parents are out for an evening, going to a party or a course of study for example. Sometimes the baby-sitter is also hired for longer periods, perhaps when the parents are away for a weekend. In such cases the "sitter" is likely to be a mature and motherly woman. For short periods, teen-age girls, college students (of either sex), nursing students, and others are commonly employed on an hourly basis.

From the point of view of convenience, the best sitter is often a girl (sometimes a boy) who lives in your apartment building or close by in the neighborhood. This gives you a chance to meet the parents and see what they are like; if an emergency occurs, the young sitter has her own mother to call upon quickly for help; you do not have to take the girl far to see her home at night or pay expensive taxi fares. Another advantage is that young people living close by can usually fill in quite readily on short notice or for short periods of time.

In an apartment house you can ask the superintendent for permission to post a notice for a baby-sitter by the mailboxes. This is often the best way to find out if there is anyone in the building who is interested in baby-sitting. Retired people as well as students are often glad to earn a little money in this way and can be found by such a note.

An excellent source is the Nursing School of a hospital. The students frequently want to earn extra money in their spare time; they have already been selected as being reliable or they would not have been accepted into the nursing school. The normal procedure is to get the telephone number of a dormitory and then call. Ask whoever answers if there is a willing baby-sitter around. Better yet, go to the school *before you need a sitter,* ask about the possibilities, and contact one or two girls, preferably on two different shifts of hours.

With any luck, you might find one or two students at a nearby college who come from your own country and speak your language. If they get to know and like you, they will come to you whenever they can.

The *disadvantage* of all students is that they are often busy in the evenings; they will not work during their holidays; and sometimes they bring along their friends. The *advantage* is that they are less expensive than anyone from an agency and, being young, are likely to be more fun for your children.

Again, if you like your cleaning woman, she herself may be willing to do some evening sitting, or she may know of someone who would like to earn a little extra money.

Other sources could be: the bulletin board of the local YWCA; the Girl Scouts sometimes organize baby-sitting services. Some

Scout Troops train older girls who earn service credits in this way. They are a particularly good possibility if you want someone to remain indoors and play with the children. Since they are young themselves, you might not want to give them outside responsibility, for example, taking children through traffic.

As you yourself make friends, don't hesitate to ask if their teenage daughters would like to baby-sit. Often they are delighted. This work is done by every kind of girl—do not be shy to ask any teenager whether or not she is available. Most mothers try to line up three or four sitters whom they (and the children) get to know and like. In this way they have alternate numbers to call in case of need.

A young couple struggling along on a tight budget—especially students—often work out an exchange agreement with another couple, "sitting" for each other's children a certain number of hours or evenings a week. The mothers exchange daytime hours as well, giving each other occasional or regular free afternoons for such things as shopping, taking a course of study, going to the hairdresser, or visiting friends.

Rates vary widely by location and age. The price for teen-agers is 75¢ to $1.25 per hour and up; for mature women or student nurses, $1.25 and up along the East Coast.

You pay more for daytime hours than evening, after the children are in bed—until midnight. After that, rates go up again. You pay more, of course, if several children are in the family. Generally you pay more if the service includes preparing or serving a meal.

If you have a small baby and want someone more responsible than a student, look under "Nurse Registries" or "Baby-Sitting Services" in the Classified Directory. If you employ the same person for many hours per month, you must pay Social Security taxes (see below) unless you get them through an agency. In that case the agency will do the paperwork for you.

CHURCH NURSERIES

Most churches have nurseries and baby-sitting services on Sunday mornings so that parents can attend services. There is usually no charge—or only a nominal one—for this service.

Many churches also run nursery schools and kindergartens during the week. Parents need not be members of the church. Some list parishioners who like to baby-sit; some have set up group baby-sitting for certain afternoons during the week so that mothers can shop or attend to other necessities.

If the local church has no facilities along these lines, they may be able to give you other suggestions.

TAXES ON HOUSEHOLD EMPLOYEES

Household employees include: cooks, cleaning women, baby-sitters, handymen, drivers, gardeners.

These rules may guide you:

If you pay any household employee $50 or more in any calendar quarter (that is, three-month period, January to March, etc.), or as little as $3.50 a week, you are *required to pay* a Social Security tax on a percent of the total wages paid. This amount may be matched by the employee—or you may pay the whole amount.

Whoever pays, you, as the employer, are responsible for mailing the total amount of tax within a month after the end of each calendar quarter to your local Internal Revenue Service (IRS) office (see telephone book under U.S. Government).

The IRS will send you a quarterly reminder to pay this tax; all you need do is write to their local office and ask for "Form 942."

If you are not now paying the taxes you owe, write the IRS explaining why you have not done so and estimate the total amount of wages you have failed to report. They will then inform you as to the amount of back taxes and interest owed. Do not delay. It is better to clear the record at once as penalties build up the longer one is overdue.

Actually, the amounts involved are not great even when you pay the full tax quarter yourself, but you can be in trouble if you do not comply with the rules.

Chapter 17

Schools in the United States

Education has been called America's religion. Today more than 56 million Americans are attending school. One half of all the people in the country between the ages of eighteen and twenty-five are enrolled in either a college or university; close to 49 million boys and girls are going to school. Education is an enormous (and expensive) part of American life; its size is matched by its variety. The widely differing educational systems and possibilities are as difficult for an outsider to understand as anything about American life.

Differences in American schools compared with those found in the majority of other countries lie in the fact that education here has long been intended for everyone—not just for a privileged elite. Schools are expected to meet the needs of every child, regardless of ability, and also of society itself. This means that tax-supported public schools offer more than academic subjects. It surprises many people when they come here to find high schools offering such courses as typing, sewing, radio repair, computer programming, or driver training, along with traditional academic subjects such as mathematics, history, and languages. Students choose their curricula from a tremendous "smorgasbord" of courses, depending on their interests, future goals, and level of ability. The underlying goal of American education is to develop every child to the utmost of his (her) own possibilities, *however great or small these may be,* and to give each one a sense of citizenship—a civic and community consciousness.

Because there is no national religion and because there are so many different backgrounds and origins among the people, the schools have traditionally been the chief institution through which a common national interest has been shared and a common heritage developed. Throughout the nineteenth and early twentieth centuries, when millions of immigrants were pouring into this country, schools played a vital part in "Americanizing" the children—and through them the parents too.

Foreigners usually notice another major difference in American schools. There is less emphasis on learning *facts* than is usual in the systems of many other countries. Instead, Americans try to teach their children to think for themselves, to delve, to explore, to develop their own intellectual and creative abilities. They spend much time learning how to use resource materials, libraries, statistics, computers. Americans believe that if a child is taught to *reason* well and to *research* well, he will be able to unearth whatever facts he needs throughout the rest of his life.

This is America's answer to the searching question that thoughtful parents all over the world are asking themselves in this fast-moving time: "How can one prepare today's child for a tomorrow that one can neither predict nor understand?"

Naturally, when any family moves from one country to another, the question of schooling for their children is always urgent and disturbing. Various choices will be open to you in the United States. Within or near whatever community you reach, there will be available to you a variety of schools—public, parochial or private; day or boarding; coeducational or all-boy/all-girl; traditional or experimental.

PUBLIC SCHOOLS

The great majority of American children attend public schools (that is, schools that are tax-supported and free). It is often confusing to people to find that there is no nationally directed standardized system for all the 50 states. Each state has been free to develop its own levels and plans. These vary so widely in quality, facilities, disciplines, and academic standards that people often move into (or out of) a state because of the level of available schooling. Men frequently take jobs—or refuse assignments—with their children's schooling in mind.

To make matters even more confusing, local school districts have considerable leeway *within* each state framework. There are tax-supported city schools and community schools which have their own patterns, boards, budgets, and standards, even though these must follow certain broad guidelines outlined by their states.

School support comes primarily from taxes at state and local levels, rather than from national funds. When the federal government does contribute to education, it does so primarily in the poorer states, where local funds are inadequate. National funds tend to be channeled for buildings, transportation, school lunch programs, or other supplements which do not affect the curriculum. As we have said above, Americans jealously guard their independence from their own national government! If there is even a chance that, as a result of accepting national funds, the government may be able to exert some kind of control, such funds are often turned down by community School Boards (elected citizens). There have been heated arguments—even riots and demonstrations at the college level—when citizens have felt that the National Government was exerting too strong an influence on some curriculum through support of scientific research programs, for example, or military training or other specific projects. "Whoever pays the piper calls the tune" says an old proverb. As much as possible, Americans raise their own funds, pay their own money, or do without a program rather than find themselves dancing to the Federal Government's tune. Since many of our forebears and many of today's new citizens have come to this country for the express purpose of escaping too much government control, this feeling still runs deep.

In line with this clear-cut separation of nation and state, there are no national examinations at either school or college levels as there are, for example, in France or England. College Board examinations, which are taken across the country for entrance to colleges and universities, are administered by a *private* organization, not by the Federal Government, and no college is compelled to use them.

The only nationally administered examinations are those ap-plying to the licensing of doctors or other professional people. Even these take place *after* they have completed their studies and are no longer university students, even at the graduate level.

One result of this state and local independence is, of course, that the quality of public education varies tremendously even from one town to the next. In our fast-growing cities, public elementary and high schools are nearly all badly overcrowded. In recent years many of them have been plagued by violence, teacher strikes, and other problems. In suburban areas and small towns, however, there are many fine public schools with excellent facilities, reasonable ra-tios between teachers and pupils, and good academic standards.

Feel free to raise questions and talk as freely as you like about schooling with any Americans you meet. Many people here are deeply concerned about the whole question of education; they con-stantly discuss the subject among themselves. They will be de-lighted to talk with you about it too. Much is good and much is bad in our current educational establishment. A great deal of change is under way; many values are being deeply reconsidered. We are in the throes of reevaluating and restructuring the whole educational system of this country in order to meet the urgent needs of this scientific twentieth century, including many new pressures from our vast and rapidly changing population.

PAROCHIAL SCHOOLS

These are the Roman Catholic counterpart to America's public school system. Not all communities have parochial schools, but most do. They, too, vary widely. They are supported not by taxes, but by the Roman Catholic Church instead. There are some fees connected with attendance at a parochial school, but these are gen-erally lower than for other private schools.

PRIVATE SCHOOLS

Private schools receive no financial support from tax funds and are—without exception—expensive. Some are more expensive than others, but all are costly and prices continue to rise rapidly.

Why do people spend so much money—often to the point of real financial sacrifice—to send their children to private schools? The reasons vary:

1) Classes tend to be smaller with greater individual attention. Some children need this kind of supportive individual instruction.
2) Most private schools are highly selective; through interviews, references, and examinations (at least for the upper levels), they seek students of quality. This means that they usually can maintain higher academic standards than the public schools which have to accept students of all abilities and carry them to the age of 16.
3) Some parents living in crowded or academically poor areas feel they must send their children to private schools if they are to be well enough prepared for admission to college.
4) A few parents prefer to send their children to schools sponsored by their own religious denominations.
5) Some parents, having class or racial prejudices, seek a more nearly homogeneous student body than is found in the public schools.

Those interested in finding out about private schools can write ahead for preliminary advice from: Advisory Service on Private Schools and Colleges, 500 Fifth Avenue, New York, N.Y. This service is free. If you write from abroad, be sure to enclose an international money order to cover return postage. If you will be in the New York area, you are welcome to visit the office after you arrive in the United States, but you can get much initial advice by mail.

In your letter include details about the kind of school in which you are interested (for example: "a boys' school in or near such-and-such a city, strong on academic preparation with the emphasis on languages" or "a small coeducational boarding school in the country for a shy fourteen-year-old girl who stutters").

Include an indication of your price range if possible, ask about scholarship possibilities, mention whether or not you prefer a church-affiliated school, indicate your preference for day or boarding, and tell how far away from your base city would be acceptable. Send along a copy of your child's school record—that is, a list of the courses taken with the grades received.

Private schools have their own admissions procedures—varying from school to school. Most of them are difficult to get into, with long waiting lists. Once you know the names of some suitable ones, write for the school catalogues, then follow their instructions regarding application for enrollment.

BOARDING SCHOOLS

These exist mostly for children of high school age though there are a few for younger children too. If you happen to settle near a boarding school, you may be able to enroll your child as a day student.

NURSERY SCHOOLS

There is such variation in preschools that it is best to wait until you arrive to see what is available in your neighborhood. Private nursery schools are often extremely expensive, but there are also informal play groups, church-affiliated nursery schools, morning programs at local YWCA's, or other possibilities in most communities which are less expensive.

Little children normally attend these for only two or three hours, once or twice a week, but they start to learn about sharing, following instructions, and being part of a group, and they enjoy companionship that otherwise is too often lacking in cities.

If you live in a housing area where there are many small children and an outdoor place to play, you probably will not need such an organized group. However, in our impersonal concrete-and-glass apartment-house world, children are sometimes lonely. In addition, those parents coming from abroad like to give their children a little extra help in learning the language and American ways before they start in the rough-and-tumble of a real school.

If you do not find a preschool that you like near your home, you may find that there are dance classes, painting sessions, swimming lessons, or other activities for little children through which you can bring your child into contact with playmates once or twice a week.

Large apartment units often provide day care or supervised play groups for little children during certain hours of the week; mothers sometimes pool their resources and take turns with each other's children in the playground partly to give themselves an occasional free afternoon and partly to give their children needed companionship.

When you are settled in your new area, you will be able to explore the possibilities near your home.

RELATIONSHIPS BETWEEN PARENT AND SCHOOL

The degree to which American parents are involved in their children's schools is often surprising to people of other countries. Most schools have organizations made up of both parents and teachers (usually called P.T.A. from the initials of the name "Parent-Teacher Association"). They meet together regularly to discuss and confer on various matters pertaining to the school—curriculum, budgets, faculty, salaries, library facilities, or whatever it may be.

Mothers often volunteer to help with classroom or after-school activities. They sometimes make costumes for plays or play the piano or assist a teacher on a class "field trip"; some of them give regular time, under the teacher's supervision, in working with slow children in the classroom.

In good schools a real effort is made to have both the home and the school work together for the child's well-being. You will generally find teachers eager to talk with you about any problems you may have concerning your child—although the larger the school (understandably), the less likely this is to happen. Where size permits, there are often "parent conferences," scheduled appointments so that parents can meet privately with one or more of their child's teachers to discuss his particular problems or progress. You will be sent notices of meetings or programs to which you are invited. Do try to go to as many as you can.

Both mothers and fathers are expected to attend such meetings and to show their interest in the school. You may be invited to a "Parents' Day" where you follow a child's schedule through a full day of classes. This is enlightening and enjoyable for most parents.

School activities provide a good way to meet your neighbors and to make friends in the community. Since Americans enjoy meeting people from other countries, you will probably find your national background a help rather than a handicap in getting acquainted. This is true even if you are having trouble with the language.

AFTER-SCHOOL OR "EXTRACURRICULAR" ACTIVITIES

In addition to their academic work, children in the United States are offered a wide range of activities in the after-school hours. These are designed to help develop their skills, abilities, and appreciations of life; to give them a chance to practice leadership and assume responsibilities; to supplement school courses; and to provide additional outlets or stimuli. There are all kinds of nature clubs, musical organizations, science clubs, art or drama groups, language clubs; a wide range of sports will be available; there will probably be a school newspaper or photography center.

Some of these activities take place during the school day, but most are held after classes are over. Even though they are optional, they are considered a real part of the American educational pattern. Parents should encourage each child to participate in whatever program best supplements his or her own special talents or interests. Much is learned in these off-duty hours, especially in terms of human "give-and-take." This after-school program is a fundamental aspect of this nation's basic educational goal, aimed at developing each student to his or her fullest potential. Americans believe this includes human relationships, social skills, and a well-trained body, as well as intellectual development.

Both employers and college admissions officers in the United States give considerable weight to the activities in which a student has participated during his free time, both after school and during his long holidays, as well as to his academic grades. This total record indicates to them something of a young person's leadership, enthusiasm, creativity, breadth of interest, vitality, and personality. They weigh these qualities together with the academic record in order to assess a student's intelligence, perseverance, and ability to *use* what he knows, rather than merely repeating it by rote on examination papers.

THE SCHOOL YEAR

For most schools the term begins in early September and ends somewhere near the middle or end of June. A few schools, generally at the high school level, also offer summer sessions. These are optional, but they give students a chance to make up work that they have missed or failed, take advance credits on extra courses they have not had time for in the school year, or just become familiar with a school before the new term starts.

Summer sessions normally hold classes in the morning, then offer a range of sports, trips, and leisure activities in the afternoon.

If you arrive in the United States in the spring with a teen-ager who plans to enter a regular school session in September, you might want to consider enrolling him or her in such a summer course to improve his English or to make friends, to gain self-confidence or perhaps just to get out of a hot city!

Most American schools have the following breakdown:

Elementary school runs from the first grade to the sixth (ages six to twelve years);

Junior high is usually grades seven and eight (ages thirteen and fourteen), although sometimes ninth grade is also included in junior high;

High school is normally grades nine through twelve (that is, fifteen years and up).

School is compulsory from the ages of six to sixteen throughout the nation.

Chapter 18

Teen-age Dating and Summers

Interrelationships among young people vary widely throughout the world. The affluence, independence, and social freedom of American youth are frightening to many parents as they contemplate bringing young people into America's teen-age world.

One of the most difficult aspects for overseas parents to accept is the fact that to a large degree youth in America sets its own rules, regulations, and patterns—parents here have less to say than in most countries about their children's actions outside the home, especially after the magic age of sixteen (the age of a driving license and often a car!). This independence is shattering to many parents from abroad who react by "forbidding" their children to take part in American teen-age activities, insisting instead that they come home directly from school and not permitting evening "dates." These dates normally include attending movies, school dances, parties at people's houses, and eating out in public places.

It is difficult for a young person to be so excluded because in the United States there are no alternatives. Virtually everyone of their age group "dates" in one way or another. This is the way the transition is made here from parental family life to marriage. It covers a long span.

There are certain things many American parents do insist upon: 1) Some set curfew hours for girls, according to their age, and expect boys to obey and bring the girls home at the appointed hour; 2) Boys also may be expected in at a reasonable hour, but must take the girl home first; 3) Parents can expect a boy to call at the front door rather than just honking his car's horn from the curb.

From eight or nine years old upward, while children are still interested in members of their own sex rather than the opposite one, they love to visit overnight in each other's houses. Little girls will have "Pajama Parties" or "Sleep-Overs." This merely means that several girls will spend the night together in one of their houses under parental supervision. There is much giggling, whispering, possibly some candy-making, pillow-fighting, and so on. It is noisy but harmless, and part of the growing-up process. Boys of the same age often want to sleep outdoors in a pup tent or tree house or on a "Camp-Out." To children of these ages, sleeping away from home marks the first stages of independence; they like to do it in groups.

The next stage is an interest in the opposite sex—first, mostly talk and giggle, then, long before they are ready emotionally or financially to marry, they start "dating."

This does not necessarily mean that they indulge in sex, despite newspaper accounts to the contrary. Although, of course, some young people do go "too far," many of them do not, despite all the talk of "The Pill," the new "hip" culture, and youth's widespread questioning of previous social patterns. Premarital chastity is no longer considered as important a virtue as it once was, but despite considerable "petting," caressing, and fondling, young people are not necessarily more sex-oriented today than they were in preceding generations.

A bigger adjustment than sex may lie in the far wider crossing of class, religious, and racial lines in young people's friendships than was true here in earlier generations or is still true in many other countries. This and the freer, more independent, and often more aggressive role of girls in America may prove to be difficult adjustments at first for many teen-agers and parents accustomed to other cultural patterns.

An interesting matter to observe is that youth generally sets, and also obeys, its own rules. These rules vary by locality and age group, but the young do set their own standards to a large degree. Those who disobey pay for it by loss of reputation, loss of popularity, or both. Most groups are quite strict within their own codes. Young people also set their own forms of dress and speech, and those within each group conform closely. Fashions vary by locality, and to some extent also by economic level and social background; fads come and go within a group, but everyone shifts at the same time and anyone who does not is likely to be dropped—or anyway ridiculed. At any large school students are likely to be able to choose from among various kinds of groups, ranging all the way from what the young call "square" (that is, clean-cut and conservative) to long-haired, bizarrely dressed, "hippie" groups. (Names and clothes may change even before this book is published, but the range of difference will remain constant.) Widely differing styles exist in most communities, each with their own manner of dress and speech. Although almost total conformity *within* each group is the rule, a young person can choose which kind of group he prefers to join.

DATING

There are three primary types of teen-age dating in "middle-class" America; the one in vogue in your community will depend on the part of the country, current local fads, and somewhat on age levels. Often all three types are carried on in the same community:

Competitive Dating

This means going out with several people during the same period, going to a dance with one, a picnic with another, a football game with a third. Sometimes two couples date together; this is known as "double-dating."

"Going Steady"

This means pairing up with one partner and doing everything with him or her—going with one another to all the parties; doing homework together; making constant telephone calls; exchanging bracelets, rings, sweaters, and so on; sometimes wearing "matching" hairdos or clothes—in short, being totally wrapped up in one another. This "steady" relationship can last anywhere from a week to several years. At the high school level it rarely leads to marriage. The breakup can be quite emotional, but generally it is *not courtship*.

Group Dating

Large groups of girl-boy pairs may go around together, sometimes shifting partners within the group, more usually not. There is almost constant physical contact such as handholding or arms draped around each other, which often frightens parents. Generally speaking, however, there is little sex in these "communal" groups at teen-age level. Growing numbers of them are, in fact, religiously oriented and extremely strict in their codes of ethics.

American parents want to see their children go out on dates. They are distressed if a daughter does not have one or more boys taking her out; they help their children in every way they can from an early age to "be popular" with the opposite sex. It is felt that through mixing easily with other young people, teen-agers gain self-assurance and experience in human relationships. The United States is a group-oriented society that rather mistrusts and somewhat pities people who prefer solitude. Parents worry if they think their child is a "loner" (that is, prefers to be by himself).

The "date"—which has only come into being since the 1900's—has therefore assumed tremendous proportions in the eyes of the young. Anyone who does not go out with the opposite sex is considered "queer" or maladjusted.

On the whole, middle-class American youth is so affluent that many people—including also many Americans—are appalled. Teen-agers, especially boys, often have their own cars; if not, they frequently are allowed to borrow the family car for "dating." Part of the reason for this goes back again to the distances in this country. Teen-agers often *must* have cars in order to get to jobs or to attend college classes or to date. Girls also expect to be driven; they do not want to walk two miles to a movie! In cities, public transportation is normally adequate of course.

The young form a tremendous consumer market, spending a great deal of money across the nation on clothes, room decorations, cars, motorcycles, snowmobiles, hi-fi's, records, and the like. The great majority of young people are responsible, hard-working and steady, despite the headlines. Unfortunately, a percentage are spoiled and irresponsible; some are insecure and deeply troubled. A high percentage of these troubled young people (as in many other countries) turn to drugs. It is well to be aware of the possible danger of drugs in your children's schools and talk about it in advance with the school principal. You will rarely find alcohol a problem among the young; they scorn it. They say "You adults get disagreeable with drink; we young get happy and relaxed with 'grass.' " Drugs are *available* at almost every school. Do not feel too frightened by this. Most young people do not choose to use drugs or use them only once or twice to experiment.

Perhaps none of this is new to you. Your home country may long since have accepted similar dating and behavior patterns. In general, however, most teen-agers around the world have more parental restrictions and restraints than do most young people in America.

The American scene can pose real problems for parents who do not want so much freedom for their young people. Those used to having their daughters "chaperoned" will find this idea rejected here. No young people would tolerate having somebody's mother "hanging around." The poor daughter would be completely cast off by her friends. Young Americans even go off now in mixed groups for unchaperoned weekends at ski lodges or on mountain hikes. They "back-pack" all over the world, camping together in hostels or dormitories or Alpine huts. But do not assume they are necessarily indulging in sex. Much of this is merely group living.

A growing trend here is toward communal recreation houses. A number of friends or families who cannot afford their own house by the sea or in the mountains where they can go for weekends or sports will contribute to buy one together. Entire families, or groups of friends, will share it communally, taking turns doing the chores, paying for their own food, apportioning the costs of taxes, repairs, or equipment. This trend may be responsible for bringing a mixture of ages back into American life. For some decades the country has been separated into clear-cut "age groups," at least in suburbia and among the more affluent elements of society. Sex usually plays no part in these shared country houses; people sleep dormitory-style.

In accord with the general trend toward sharing and equality between the sexes, more and more girls pay some or part of their way on dates, especially if they have as much money as the boy. This is often called "going Dutch Treat." Since girls are becoming more aggressive, it is no longer uncommon nowadays for them to initiate a date.

Despite worries over teen-age morality in this open society, parents may find much that is good in the system too. The depth and freedom of discussion, the vitality and initiative, the sense of public and community service, the easy camaraderie of American youth, can provide great experiences for young visitors. The newcomers will inevitably take part in life with their school friends. One should not try to prevent this. If they are made to seem "queer" or different" by parental decree, they may become very lonely for they will be cut off by their schoolmates.

Parents can exert an *indirect* influence, however. First, of course, they have the all-important choice of neighborhood and school. In addition they can encourage, in an inconspicuous way, certain of their children's friendships more than others; they can provide outside activities with different young people—ski trips, for example, or volunteer projects or a photography class or summer excursions. Parents should get to know their child's school and other parents; join the Parent-Teacher group; attend all school functions; offer your services on any school committees. The more you take part in the school life, the more you will understand your child and his friends.

SUMMER CAMPS AND JOBS

Camps

Partly because of summer heat but mostly because we began as an agricultural nation, summer holidays are very long. Children and youth get restless if they are idle for too long, especially when they are living in cramped city apartments. As a result there are thousands of different kinds of summer camps for children—specialty ones like music or riding or tennis camps; water or mountain camps; day or live-in ones; cheap or expensive. Most run for eight weeks; often, however, you can find two-week or four-week camps if you prefer. Some are Scout-run, others YM or YWCA-supported. Private camps are costly but provide horses, team sports, canoe trips, or a variety of experiences.

Older teen-agers are more likely to seek summer jobs or go off with their own age groups on camping or other trips, perhaps exploring the West or taking student tours abroad if they can afford it.

Jobs

Many teen-agers earn a good portion of their college fees by working during their summer vacations at all kinds of jobs—waitress or deck hand or harvester; construction worker, camp counselor, or mother's helper; telephone operator or soda fountain clerk. They are not concerned with status. Being unskilled, they try to find jobs at whatever level they can, doing however much they can. They seek not only money, but also experience. They learn work habits, responsibility, the ability to take orders and to get on with a boss and new kinds of people. As they grow older and more competent, most of them get better jobs, probably still unskilled but more closely tied to their fields of interest—in hospitals, political headquarters, newspapers, schools, or wherever. Students from abroad should check carefully into visa regulations if they also want to use the long holidays in this way. The Dean or Foreign Student Advisor at any school or college should be able to offer advice here, but the visa question should be raised in one's home country before leaving.

One should not come to America worried about one's children. The overwhelming majority of American young people are serious-minded and clean-spirited. However, undeniably, in this troubled world, youth is restless everywhere; problems do arise. Since American parents as well as visitors are naturally concerned about any difficulties their children may be experiencing, there are many sources of advice and guidance in this country, all of which are freely available to any parent. If you are concerned, you will be able to ask advice. Nearly all schools, for example, have what are known as "Guidance Counselors." It is the job of these men or women to advise either students or parents who are perplexed or insecure in any way. It might be wise for you and your children to go together to talk with your school's counselor soon after your arrival, well *before* there are any problems. Ask the counselor about the local dating situation, school activities, all the various possibilities and patterns in both the community and school. Then you can *plan* your choices instead of just finding your way by chance.

Ministers, priests, or rabbis are also available to advise those who wish to consult them in terms of a particular community.

An excellent background book (to which we are much indebted) is *American Youth Culture: Group Life in Teen-age Society* by Ernest A. Smith, Professor of Sociology at Hunter College in New York (The Free Press of Glencoe, New York).

Most public libraries have "young adult" sections. Librarians will help you to find useful information along these lines if you ask their aid. As in every other phase of adjusting to this new culture, you should feel free to ask those around you for their ideas and advice. Parents are everywhere; you will find them interested in your thoughts, your problems, and your reactions to the whole picture of teen-age youth. They will not be embarrassed to discuss the subject, and you need feel no hesitation either. Most of the world is going through deep social changes and moral questioning. Nowhere is this more true—or more perplexing—than in the attitudes and actions of teen-aged youth. Your neighbors, friends, and business colleagues will welcome the chance to share this concern with you and exchange ideas.

Chapter 19

Religion—In and Out of Church

In large cities it is possible to find places of worship for most of the major faiths, including Moslem mosques and Hindu or Buddhist temples. This reflects again the variety of people from all over the world who now make their homes in the United States. However, rather understandably, in smaller towns or rural areas, you will in all probability find only Christian churches (of numerous denominations) and Jewish synagogues.

Especially in small towns, churches are centers for much social and community life. Here you will find such activities as church suppers, dances, discussion groups, sports and social get-togethers, youth programs, and the like. Although you will not be given a personal invitation to these events, you will be welcome at any of them; they are held for the express purpose of including everyone in the life of the church. Increasing numbers of people now come from other lands. Church groups welcome you, regardless of your faith.

If you do not see a church of your own faith near your new home, turn to the Classified Directory under "Churches." If you find a church you like and want to attend regularly, just introduce yourself to the minister and tell him your wishes. He will welcome you, will help you to meet people and advise you about any "settling-in" problems you may have.

Our churches offer so much in the way of social life that some people find it overwhelming. No one need take part in any more than he or she wants to. People may urge you, in the desire to make you feel welcome. But if you prefer to participate only in the worship services, do not feel that you are obligated to do more. It is a completely personal choice. The types of activities you will find most churches offer in addition to the services often include: nursery schools for little children; after-school programs for older ones; lunches, discussion groups, or voluntary work for women; men's outings or breakfasts; concerts and plays.

Many churches hold "Coffee Hours" after the Sunday morning service. These are completely informal and friendly. Anyone who wants to just drifts into the Parish House for coffee and cake. You have some refreshment, chat with anybody you see there, and leave again whenever you want. It is a pleasant, easy way to meet people of the neighborhood.

Chapter 20

Finding Friends and Having Fun

THE LAND OF LEISURE TIME?

American workers keep demanding and getting shorter and shorter working hours; they are now discussing the prospect of a four-day work week. Numbers of firms are in fact already trying the shorter week. Since machines have speeded up work in homes as well as factories, both men and women have more free time than ever before in our history. Because Americans play hard and rather loudly, a visitor's first impression may be one of mass holidaying— of camper-trucks rolling down the highways, crowded beaches, packed baseball stadiums, endless television. In order to understand the true picture of how Americans use their leisure, however, one needs to look below this noisy surface.

It is true of course that much leisure is used in play. It is a country of sports—hunting and fishing, swimming, sailing, and golfing are available at all prices to all levels of workers. Americans by the million love both to play and to watch team sports like baseball or football. They bowl, roller skate, ski, or follow active sports of every kind. Also, by the million, they watch television, take part in community orchestras, make their own films or recordings, go camping, travel, garden, read books, and pursue many other crafts and hobbies. Being part of a "do-it-yourself" country, people enjoy building their own shelves or boats, sewing their own clothes, developing their own photographs; they do such things for fun as well as for economy.

This is a "self-improvement" country too. More than 25 million adults are enrolled in one kind of course or another, mostly on their own time, at their own expense.

VOLUNTEERING

But in addition to the time spent on personal pursuits, Americans volunteer a tremendous amount of time for the varied needs of their communities. It has been said that "If all the volunteers of the country withdrew, the nation would come to a halt." This would include hospitals, many schools, libraries, museums, playgrounds, community centers, welfare projects, clinics, and so on.

Why do so many Americans work long, hard hours, often at dull and disagreeable work, without pay? What is their motive? Why do they do it?

There are several answers. The concept of cooperating for mutual benefit, a sense of interlocking responsibility, a willingness to work together, have all been deeply rooted here since the country's founding. It was imperative. The original pioneer settlers had to work together to survive. They had crossed dangerous seas and risked all they had in their struggle for political and religious liberation. We have seen that much of that deep-seated distrust of central government remains and crops out in all aspects of American life. People still prefer to do things themselves within their communities, rather than give a government agency control or wait for its bureaucratic delays.

Sometimes volunteering results because Americans want to achieve something for which no money is paid. So they come together to contribute their energies—as is done in many lands. They may work together to put a new roof on a church, to send parcels to flood victims, to provide summer holidays for underprivileged children, or to clean up a polluted stream. Men will give time after a long hard day to work on a Town Zoning Commission or School Board or Planning Committee. They care about their town. Women have been freed of many hours of housework by the multitude of prepackaged, perma-prest, and disposable items now available.

Some of them use this leisure for volunteering because they are lonely or bored at home; others because they are genuinely interested in the work; others from a sense of duty or because they are learning from the experience or because it is the acceptable thing to do.

Whatever the reason, hundreds of thousands of so-called leisure hours (as a result of America's short work week) go into hard, sustained, unpaid work on one or another community need. As you read the local newspapers, you will see that Americans are constantly forming new kinds of citizens' groups: to improve the lot of migrant workers; to take action against some form of discrimination; to fight crime; to elect an official; to protect consumers from fraud; to do away with a pesticide that is killing wildlife.

One does not need to be a citizen to join in such activities. Once you settle into a community (even a big city), you will soon be aware of the varieties of voluntary work that are going on around you. Anyone who is interested in sharing this side of American life will greatly deepen his understanding of the country. All you need do is let your interest be known and people will show you where to start.

DO YOU ALREADY BELONG?

Perhaps in your home country you already belong to some group such as Rotary, Lions, YWCA, university women—or to a professional group (journalists, chemical engineers, doctors, and so on). Perhaps you belong to a sports club—ski, tennis, soccer, or hiking —or a university alumni group. (Many overseas universities have alumni chapters scattered around the United States.)

If you are already a member of any such organization at home, look for its affiliate here and let them know of your desire to participate. You will get an immediate welcome. If you are interested in, but not yet affiliated with, any such group, try to become a member before leaving your own country. You will then automatically be eligible to join activities with your American counterparts on arrival without waiting for long membership formalities. Such channels for making new friends will be most useful when you first arrive, so it is good to come with introductions and with memberships already established if you can.

INTEREST GROUPS

There are of course many sports and activities which anyone can do without joining formal groups. Hunters and fishermen can find colleagues here in great numbers, as can climbers, hikers, or skiers; so can bridge players, photographers, chess enthusiasts, bird watchers, or cello players! Whatever your nationality, you can also find a national group in any large city. Ask at your nearest consulate or look under "Associations" in the Classified Directory to find the Turkish Society, India House, African Center, or whatever exists locally.

Mah-jongg or chess players, stamp collectors, those who seek a small informal orchestra, or others with special interests should ask their friends, neighbors, and office colleagues where to find such groups. Every locality has them; often the local librarian can give you leads or you will find them listed under "Clubs" in the telephone book (Classified). Language problems would hardly bother you at all in any such gatherings. Rarely are such clubs "exclusive"; generally they are eager for new and interested members, so do not feel shy to explain that you have just arrived from another country and are looking for people who share your interest and enthusiasm.

You will find that expressed eagerness to take part in almost anything will open all kinds of doors to you. Americans like active, energetic people. This is the way we ourselves meet each other as we keep moving to new communities within our own country. Out of such shared interests come invitations into people's homes and thus gradually into the real life of any locality.

HAVE YOU ALWAYS MEANT TO STUDY?

Perhaps for a while when you first come to America you will want to study English—or to join an English conversation group in order to gain confidence in speaking.

Or perhaps you will have time to acquire some new skills, to take a short course that has always interested you or finish one that needs to be completed.

One secretary at the United Nations took a stenotyping course in her free evenings. By the time she returned home to Malaysia she was able to command twice her previous salary by expert reporting of meetings and conferences; later she opened a small stenotyping school in her own country and again more than doubled her salary!

Adult education is widespread. Classes are offered in every known thing: painting, cooking, photography, languages, astronomy, being a travel agent, programming computers. One need not necessarily have any particular qualifications to enroll in such classes or to learn new skills.

Some people may be interested in taking more substantive and longer courses leading to degrees, certificates, or diplomas of various kinds. Possibilities include such a range as: journalism, interior decorating, fashion design, business administration, accounting, and so on.

Both classes and courses are advertised in local newspapers, especially on Sundays and at the change of terms (that is, September, January, or June). Look under "Schools" in the telephone book (Classified). YM and YWCA's offer a wide range of classes; the public school systems of most cities sponsor various adult evening classes. Ask for a catalogue of adult courses from the local Board of Education.

In addition, if you are near any of the nation's 1,800 colleges and universities, you will find they make available varied courses, concerts, and lectures to the nearby community. Usually these are held in the evening; you can ask to be put on their mailing list for advance notices.

LECTURES

Americans love lectures! If you like to be mentally stimulated but do not have time for a complete course, you can follow any line of interest on a more casual basis—often free. Or you may want to explore new fields like oceanography, city planning, or outer space!

In addition to lectures given at colleges and universities, you will find that botanical gardens, civil rights organizations, government and political groups, churches, and museums also offer a great number of lectures, debates, and forums; so do international organizations, business groups, and professional bodies.

Get yourself on mailing lists (usually free for the asking), listen to local radio announcements, or ask your friends' advice. Easiest of all—just read the newspapers!

MUSEUMS CAN BE ENGROSSING

If your idea of a museum is a dusty, musty row of glass cases or rooms full of miserably lit oil paintings, try afresh! The art of display itself has become highly developed in this country so that museums have come "alive" in the past years to an extraordinary degree.

In addition to many fine art museums, look also for natural history museums. Photographic exhibits are often a particularly good way to understand the social concerns of a country. Don't miss the many small museums of contemporary crafts, Negro history, American Indian history, musical instruments, coins. While at the museum one can often rent a small tape-recorded guide which adds much to one's understanding (rental fees range from 35 cents to about $1 for two or three hours). In bigger cities these are sometimes provided in several languages as well. Those going to Boston,

New York, Philadelphia, Washington, D.C., Atlanta, Chicago, Denver, or San Francisco should plan to spent considerable time in the particularly fine museums of these cities.

DO YOU LIKE THEATER? MUSIC?

The country abounds in these arts, both professional and amateur. Most cities have their own symphony orchestras; there is a wealth of experimental, offbeat drama being produced across the country in college theaters, community centers, and small neighborhood theaters.

Theater

Ticket prices for legitimate theater in the big cities have soared; so have the prices of movies in major theaters. However, you can avoid these by going to smaller theaters which often have the same performances, but at lower prices. Many cities now subsidize a City Center, keeping prices at a reasonable level; ask New Yorkers about "twofers"—meaning two tickets for the price of one. Sometimes at the end of a long and successful Broadway run, or when promoters are trying to fill a faltering house for an unknown artist, these become available. Often you can use them to see excellent productions at half price.

Theater, opera, and concert tickets are often hard to come by— partly because the population of cities is mushrooming; partly because public taste is growing more and more arts-minded. There are various ways to obtain tickets—besides the usual one of going to the box office weeks in advance.

Read the theater reviews in local newspapers, then *write in* quickly for tickets, sending a check or money order with your request. This is the best way if you have lots of time; but be *sure* to send a *self-addressed and stamped* envelope or you will get no answer. If you can offer two or three dates, your chance of getting one of them is far better than if you specify only one. Sometimes all the

tickets in the house are taken over on a given night for a charity or
special "outing." So give alternate dates if you possibly can, and
write as far ahead as practical.

If theater is important to you, you can join a "theater club" in
most cities and get tickets through them. They usually open their
membership (normally $5 to $10 for a season) in September. Watch
the theater section of the newspapers for advertisements. They send
members reviews of plays before they open, as well as giving them
the chance to buy tickets by mail in advance at reduced rates.

Music

Almost your only hope of getting tickets for opera and major
concerts in most cities is to take out a season ticket, by subscrip-
tion. Look into this long before September 1, if you can. Renewals
are offered to old subscribers in June, then series go on public sale.
As these are apt to be expensive, it is quite usual for several people
to join together to buy one "series." They then divide the tickets
among themselves, each couple going once or twice a month. This
is perfectly legitimate and often done.

Another method of securing tickets for a particular performance
is to do it through ticket brokers. You pay (legally) $1.50 more per
ticket. These brokers handle about 5 percent of all theater and concert tickets sold in a big city like New York.

You will find brokers in the telephone directory (Classified)
under "Theater Brokers" or "Theater Tickets." You will also find
them at desks in the lobbies of most good hotels and clustered
around the theater district.

WHAT ABOUT SPORTS?

Newcomers to the United States often find lack of exercise and
sports one of their hardest adjustments. Actually, it need not be so.
Almost all sports are available in (or near) cities, even in a city such
as New York with all its mortar, steel, and glass. One of the first

places to investigate if you are interested in swimming, tennis, badminton, gym classes, modern dance, or anything of an indoor sport nature is the nearest YM or YWCA. Most of these are well equipped and provide excellent facilities for reasonable fees. There are fancier and more expensive facilities for all such sports in most cities as well.

Swimming

A great many swimming pools are open to the public. In addition to those run by the YW or YMCA, others are operated by the cities themselves or by hotels or swimming schools. When weather permits, there are often public and private beaches available within easy distance. Usually these are linked with the city by public transport—either bus or train—as well as by private car. Look in the telephone book under "Swimming."

Other Sports

Read the newspapers or look in the telephone book under the name of whatever sport interests you, and you will find: ski trips (day or weekend), walking clubs, fencing, gymnasiums, judo and karate classes, ice skating, squash and rackets, bicycle clubs, riding groups, bird watchers. One of this country's favorite sports is bowling. In addition to private clubs, nearly all cities maintain numerous tennis courts and golf courses which are open to the public for small fees. Ask your local Department of Parks for booklets describing their sports facilities. In New York, for example, one can join in soccer games, cricket, field hockey—even "curling"!

Those who like baseball need only drift around the parks. Many games will be going on; usually they need and welcome additional players.

Camping and Hiking

Within relatively easy access (by bus or car), one will find excellent camping facilities in both state and national parks.

One can get free booklets and maps describing camp facilities and park areas by writing either to the individual state or to the National Parks Department. It is advisable to get information from both by addressing:

State: Department of Parks, State Capitol, State (as appropriate for your state);

National: National Parks Department, Department of the Interior, Washington, D.C.

In addition, ask at any good sports store for local information. The salesmen are likely to know all the nearby resources well.

All over the United States, there are thousands of miles of walking trails, all kinds of lodges and huts, and a great many campsites where you can pitch tents and find water, but you need to know where to find them in order to avoid overcrowded highways, hot dog stands, and too many people. The above two sources will get you started if you are woods- and camp-minded. You will need to make reservations well ahead of time in most of these public areas; one of the disadvantages of our vast size and population is that we must schedule solitude!

Fishing and Hunting

The state and national booklets described above also include information for the fisherman and hunter. In addition you can always find fellow enthusiasts in your own locality. Talk to your colleagues; read the sports columns in the newspapers; chat with salesmen in the sports stores. Through such contacts, you can find out what clubs there are in the vicinity and then ask about the possibility of joining one. Public-owned facilities are likely to be crowded; joining a group or club gives you access to more private waters and woods. Most clubs have reasonably open membership rules and would welcome your inquiry. They range in price from moderate to high; the lower the price the more welcoming they are in general, but also, of course, the more crowded. The expensive clubs are, of course, likely to be the most exclusive.

Birds

Those interested in birds should look up the nearest Audubon Society in the telephone book and ask about groups, activities, or sanctuaries that exist in the area.

Deep-Sea Fishing

Deep-sea fishermen will find boats and salty old captains ready to take them out at almost any marina or port. Prices per day are high, but you can avoid this if you make up a group and go together, thus dividing the cost among many of you.

MEETING FAMILIES AT HOME

Many countries have developed programs for visiting travelers enabling them to meet families in their country. America has a similar program. You can have an interesting experience if you write to: U.S. Travel Service, Department of Commerce, Washington, D.C. 20025. Ask for their free brochure called *Meet Americans at Home*. In it you will find telephone numbers and names listed for local offices in many (but not all) cities across the United States. You describe your interests; they will then arrange an invitation for you, doing their best to "match" you with a congenial family. This may take a day or two to arrange, but you will then be invited for a meal or out for a drive or perhaps for an evening visit after dinner.

There is no fee for this—the host family has volunteered and it is their pleasure to invite you—but it is nice to take some small hostess gift with you, as a friendly gesture, and of course to write a note of thanks afterwards.

WATCHING AMERICANS AT WORK

There are many people who do not want to become deeply involved with American activities but who still are interested in

learning about the country. They are welcome to "watch the wheels
go round" if they so desire. It is easy to watch a nation work when
you visit people at their jobs.

If you cannot find out about possibilities through your friends,
just call the place of business that most interests you (factory, bank,
police training school, or whatever). Ask for the Public Relations
Department. They will be able to tell you whether they have tours
or whether you can visit independently. Tell them where you are
from and why you are interested. In most cases you will find that
people are friendly and pleased to have you visit as their guest, although they first may check with your office to make sure you are
bona fide. Do not tip or pay any fee, but a thank-you letter afterward would be much appreciated.

You can visit most kinds of factories and watch men and women
working at heavy industry, precision work, food-processing; you
can call on various kinds of schools; watch courts in progress; listen to hearings before government committees; attend town meetings, zoning meetings, or school boards. Rarely are any of these
private; usually the public is admitted although only by previous
arrangement. You can often go aboard ocean liners in the big
ports; often there are tours for the public "behind the scenes" in
such places as department stores, post offices, or newspaper plants.

The thing to remember in this country is not to be shy or retiring.
We welcome guests; we are flattered to have people interested in
what we are doing; we are proud to show them what we have. The
secret, however, is to make arrangements in advance; be sure your
visit will be convenient to the other person; then be *on time.* If you
are going to be late or find that you are prevented from going, *telephone in advance to let them know.*

The thing that distresses busy people is to make plans and take
trouble for someone and then find it was all in vain and unappreci-
ated. Everyone knows that accidents and emergencies sometimes
prevent people from coming. But this is a telephone land. We do
not understand when (as often happens) the overseas guest does not
phone to say he is sorry, that he has been detained or cannot come.

To us it is really rude to omit this simple courtesy and consideration.

This country is yours—full of variety, full of welcome. It is so big and moves at so swift a pace that it can pass you by if you do not stretch out your hands to it. But anyone who wants to join in its mainstream and is not shy to make himself (or herself) known to the people around him will find a ready welcome. You will have more to do than time to do it in once you begin!

We are glad you are coming; we hope your experiences here will be rich and happy.

Appendix

Dull but Important Formalities

VISAS

If you are not planning to settle permanently in the United States, you are likely to be classified as a "non-immigrant" alien. This means that to enter the country you will need a visa as well as a passport and health record.

There are various kinds of visas depending on the estimated length of stay and, even more important, the purpose and auspices of the visit. (Canadians, British residents of Canada, and Mexicans who have Border Crossing cards do not need visas.)

To get a visa, you present your passport to the nearest U.S. Consulate.

Among types of visas available are:

B 1, B 2

Normal short visits for business = B 1
Normal short visits for pleasure = B 2

With either of these, you may not work for pay.

F 1, F 2

Student = F 1
Family of student = F 2

J 1, J 2

Exchange visitor on a State Department program = J 1
Spouse or children of exchange visitor = J 2

H 1

For aliens coming temporarily who are of distinguished merit and ability, usually entertainers, sports stars, lecturers, etc., offering services of an exceptional nature.

H 2

Aliens coming for short-term special work with skills not readily available in the United States.

H 3

Industrial trainees coming to the U.S. for training in work they will return to do abroad on completion of program.

A small white form, 1-94, will be stapled into your passport which will show the classification under which you arrived, the arrival date, the purpose of the visit, and (most important) the departure date assigned to you by the U.S. Immigration and Naturalization Service. If you want to stay longer than the date on this form, you must apply for an "Extension of Stay" *at least one month* before the expiration date. Ask at the nearest Immigration and Naturalization Service office for the necessary form to fill out.

Don't let your visa expire by mistake! You would be surprised how many people do. If you overstay your date without an approved extension, you will find yourself going through enormous amounts of red tape.

ALIEN REGISTRATION

If you are over twenty-one years old and in the United States past the turn of any calendar year (January 1st), you must fill out a short alien registration card (1-53) during the month of January. This applies to each member of a family over twenty-one. The purpose of this form is merely to give the Department of Justice a yearly check on the addresses of aliens. Forms can be had at any post office. There is no charge. Just ask for them at the counter during the month of January. If you fail to do this, you could be deported.

TAXES*

Those working for a corporation will be advised about taxes by their firm; others should consult a tax expert in their bank or a lawyer. Avoid the "tax advisors" who advertise in the streets; many of these are not reliable. Go to someone you can trust.

There are certain tax facts which are helpful to know:

In the United States most people pay at least two forms of Income Tax: Federal and State. In some areas they also pay a City Tax. Even if you live in one state, you may pay the tax of another if you earn your money there. For example: people who live in New Jersey or Connecticut pay a New York City tax on what they earn in that city; they also pay a New York State tax.

A booklet, *U.S. Tax Guide for Aliens*, has been published and is available for·30¢ through the Internal Revenue Service Office in the area where you settle. Or you can write for it by addressing Superintendent of Documents, U.S. Government Printing Office, Washington, D.C. 20402. Enclose 30¢ by check or money order, not stamps or cash.

Anyone who has been in the country for 90 days in one year or who has earned over $3,000 in one year should check to see if he is liable for payment of taxes. He should also find out whether or not he is covered by a treaty between the United States and his home country. Some countries have such treaties which grant certain exemptions from U.S. taxes. The normal rule is that a person is liable for taxation by only one country, his own or the United States, but not both. Not all countries have such agreements, however. Be sure to know about your own. You can get this information from your embassy or consulate or from the nearest U.S. one. Even when such agreements do exist, the details vary. Some countries will refund some of the taxes paid in the United States, but you may have to pay first and argue later!

* (Information courtesy of Mr. Henry A. Schloemer, Chief Review Staff (Acting) of District Director of Internal Revenue Service, New York, N.Y.)

Filing Dates

If you are being taxed as a "non-resident alien" and you have no wages subject to withholding, you file your income tax return *on or before June 15.*

If your status is "resident alien" for income tax purposes, or if you are a "non-resident alien" but you are receiving wages that are subject to withholding, you must file *on or before April 15.*

Even if you do not have to actually pay any tax, you will almost surely need to file a return. Ask, ask, ask! It is better to be sure than sorry.

As in all bureaucracies, you may get a bit of a run-around or be kept waiting or have to fill out a great many forms. Bear with it; in the long run these people are trying to help you with your tax questions before problems or penalties arise.

Before Leaving the United States

Before returning home, you will have to satisfy the U.S. Internal Revenue Service that your taxes have been paid. To obtain a Sailing (or exit) Permit you will need to fill out Form 1040C or Form 2063.

You will be asked to submit this form together with:

1) Your passport;
2) Alien registration card (if you have one);
3) Copy of any previous year's returns and proof of tax paid (if you have this);
4) Statement from your employer as to wages earned and taxes already paid;
5) Report of any other income in the current year on which there is no withholding (if you made speeches, or wrote articles, for example);
6) Any other records and documents such as receipts, bank records, canceled checks, etc., that substantiate business expenses.

ELIGIBILITY FOR MILITARY SERVICE

Those entering the country with a non-immigrant visa are no longer required to register with the military authorities. Immigrant aliens, however, are still subject to military draft if they are male, under the age of twenty-six, and have lived in the United States for one year.

Since requirements are likely to change with the world situation, it is well to telephone the local draft board for up-to-date rulings on this if you are in the eligible category. Look under "U.S. Government—Selective Service" in the local telephone book.

WHAT YOU CAN BRING THROUGH CUSTOMS*

You may be asking yourself "What can I bring into the United States without paying duty?" "Can I bring gifts?" "Must I declare *everything?*" "Is there anything that I may not bring?"

You should obtain a copy of a pamphlet, *Customs Hints for Visitors (Nonresidents)*, giving full answers to all such questions from the nearest U.S. Consulate. In brief, Customs regulations for visitors to the United States include:

Personal Belongings

If the items are for your own use and not for sale, you may bring in without duty or tax any items of a personal nature. These include clothes, jewelry, toilet articles, cameras, sports equipment.

Household Goods

Furniture, rugs, linens, books, professional equipment or instruments, china, glassware, etc., may all come in with you without Customs duty if:

* (Information courtesy of Mr. Charles E. McGee, Special Assistant for Public Affairs to the Commissioner, Bureau of Customs, Department of the Treasury, New York.)

1) They are for your own use;
2) You are not intending to sell them;
3) They have been used for at least a year in the household where you were a resident member.

(This does not include machinery of any sort, nor theatrical props, scenery, or costumes.)

Antiques

If these arrive separately from your household goods, you should have proof of their age. They can enter free if they are over 100 years old or if they are part of your household.

Time of Shipment

All these various goods need not come with you; you can have them shipped later if you prefer. If they arrive *before* you do, they will collect duties which you will have to pay to claim them. However, you can have this money refunded in full afterward by applying for a refund to the District Director of Customs. Ask for the proper forms when you pay the charges, and be sure to keep your ticket (air or ship) to prove the date of your entry.

It is advisable to have any documents or papers photocopied before sending them to an official so that you have a full, exact replica for your own files.

Cars, Bicycles, Motorcycles, etc.

If you enter these with your other goods upon arrival, owned them or ordered them before you left home, and do not sell them for a year, you may bring them in duty-free. If you sell before the year, you will have to pay the duty prior to the sale (at the nearest Customs Office).

Pets

Cats, dogs, monkeys, etc., must meet certain requirements before they may enter. Ask at the nearest U.S. Consulate for the booklet *So You Want to Import a Pet* or write:

Foreign Quarantine Program
U.S. Public Health Service
National Communicable Disease Center
Atlanta, Georgia 30333

Gifts

You may bring in up to $100 worth of gifts providing you spend at least 72 hours in the United States and you have not claimed this gift provision or any part of it within the previous six months.

One gallon of alcoholic beverages and 100 cigars may be included within this gift exemption for travelers over twenty-one years of age.

Alcohol, Cigarettes, Tobacco

One quart of alcohol per adult may enter free; also duty-free are 300 cigarettes or 50 cigars or three pounds of smoking tobacco (not Cuban) or a proportion of each.

(*Note:* One may always bring in more than the exempt amount of any of the above—just be prepared to pay duty on the excess.)

Not Allowed

Some things may *not* be brought into the United States without special permits:

1) *Drugs*

If you must bring in a special prescription, be *sure* to get a permit in advance. Inquire at the U.S. Consulate for details.

2) *Plants*

Any kind whatsoever of fruits, vegetables, plants, seeds, cuttings, or plant products—not even one apple!

If you want to bring them in, you must write *ahead* for permission from:

Import and Permit Section
Plant Quarantine Division
209 River Street
Hoboken, New Jersey 07030

The reason for this ruling is that the country is desperately trying to prevent insects or plant diseases from being brought in by mistake.

3) *Meats and Hides*

For the same reason, to avoid animal diseases, one cannot bring in meats (including sausages, salamis, etc.); no untanned furs or hides; no cattle, horses, burros, etc.; no wildfowl or barnyard fowl (including eggs for hatching!).

If you wish to bring them in, write to:

Animal Health Division
U.S. Agricultural Research Service
Hyattsville, Maryland 20782

4) *Goods from Certain Countries*

One cannot import goods of any kind originating in North Korea, North Vietnam, or Cuba; goods brought from China must be for personal use or gifts or have a special entry license.

Inquiries should be made to:

Foreign Assets Control
Department of the Treasury
Washington, D.C. 20220

5) *Gold*

There are tight restrictions regarding gold, gold coins, gold coin jewelry or medals.

6) *Firearms and Ammunition*

You may bring guns and ammunition for sporting purposes only, but solely with import permission from:

Firearms Division
Internal Revenue Service
Washington, D.C. 20224

No ammunition, pistols, or revolvers may be shipped in the U.S. mails.

Questions

If you have questions on Customs regulations that cannot be answered by your nearest U.S. Embassy or Consulate, write:

Bureau of Customs
Department of the Treasury
Washington, D.C. 20226

Household Helps

CENTIGRADE AND FAHRENHEIT

To change Centigrade into Fahrenheit multiply by 9/5 and then add 32.

You may find it easier to learn a few of the most common temperature measures by heart!

CENTIGRADE	FAHRENHEIT
−18°	0°
0°	32°
10°	50°
20° (room temp.)	68°
30°	86°
40°	104°
100° (boiling)	212°

Body temperature: 36.9°C is 98.6°F.

METRICS AND AMERICAN MEASURES

Practically all the world measures by the metric system but as yet the United States has not adopted it, though we plan to do so someday! To give you some shortcuts to learning the American system:

Kilometer This is just over $\frac{1}{2}$ *mile* (literally $\frac{6}{10}$ of a mile); multiply kilometers by .6 to get miles.

Kilogram Think of this as two *pounds,* though actually it is 2.2 pounds. (A "stone," the British measure of weight, is 14 pounds or 6.3 kg.)

Meter Think of it as just over a *yard*—literally $\frac{11}{10}$ of a yard. One U.S. *foot,* which is 12 inches, is 30.4 centimeters; one meter is 3.2 feet.

Centimeter If you think of this as $\frac{1}{2}$ *inch*, you are not far off for everyday purposes (although it is actually $\frac{3}{10}$ of an inch, not $\frac{5}{10}$); 91 centimeters is one U.S. *yard.*

Liter Think of it as a *quart* (actually $\frac{11}{10}$ of a quart); you buy gasoline by the *gallon*, which is four quarts.

Gram This is so small that you will seldom meet it here; it takes 30 grams to make one *ounce*, which is the smallest commonly used measure in everyday life. There are 16 ounces in a pound.

CLOTHING SIZES

Changes are being made in varying degrees throughout the world as countries attempt to standardize sizes. However, there is still so much variation that shopping is always difficult when one first moves to another land.

Even with a size-conversion chart, you would do well to shop with your tape measure in hand and, above all, try clothing on. Shapes, fullness, armholes, proportion of body size to neckband or sleeve length vary according to national origin. If your size is not "standard" by American measures, you may have to search a bit among unfamiliar terms such as "Junior Miss" or "Petite," "King Size" or "Stout Size" or "Out Size." Large department stores often have what they call "Personal Shopping Departments" or "Service Desks" where you can get help if you ask for it. Many major stores in large cities have salespeople who can speak a number of languages.

The following comparison of American with European sizes may be helpful to Asians, Africans, or South Americans as well, since many countries follow either British or Continental measures. Please realize, however, that there is much variation from country to country and even within countries as well. The information below, therefore, is included only as a guide and is not to be taken as necessarily an exact measure.

WOMEN

Dresses and Coats—Misses

U.S.A.	8	10	12	14	16	18	20
British	—	10	12	14	16	18	20
Continental	—	38	40	42	44	46	48

Dresses and Coats—*Women's*

U.S.A.	34	36	38	40	42	44
British	34	36	38	40	42	44
Continental	42	44	46	48	50	52

Dresses and Coats—*Junior*

U.S.A. and British	7	9	11	13	15	17
Continental	34	35	38	40	42	44

Stockings

U.S.A. and British	8	$8\frac{1}{2}$	9	10	$10\frac{1}{2}$	11
Continental	0	1	2	4	5	6

(But many European countries also use the same as the U.S.A.)

Blouses, Sweaters, Slips

U.S.A. and British	30	32	34	36	38	40
Continental	38	40	42	44	46	48

Shoes

U.S.A.	5	$5\frac{1}{2}$	6	7	8	$8\frac{1}{2}$	9
British	$3\frac{1}{2}$	4	$4\frac{1}{2}$	$5\frac{1}{2}$	$6\frac{1}{2}$	7	$7\frac{1}{2}$
Continental	35	35	36	38	$38\frac{1}{2}$	39	40

MEN

Coats and Suits

U.S.A.	36	38	40	42	44	46
European	46	48	50	54	56	59

Shirts

U.S.A.	$14\frac{1}{2}$	15	$15\frac{1}{2}$	16	$16\frac{1}{2}$
European	37	38	39	40	41

Shoes and Slippers

U.S.A.	8	$8\frac{1}{2}$	$9\frac{1}{2}$	10	$10\frac{1}{2}$
European	41	42	43	44	45

Americans often use the sizes Small, Medium, Large, or Extra Large.

FOR WOMEN:

Small	Sizes under 12;
Medium	Sizes 14–16 and sometimes also 12;
Large	18 and up; sometimes also 16.

In skirts, dresses, coats, half sizes are usually intended for the short-waisted, stocky figure.

FOR MEN:

Small	Sizes under 36 British or American or 46 European;
Medium	36–38 British or 46–48 European;
Large	40 British, 50 European; anything over is *Extra Large.*

TRANSLATING COOKING MEASURES

Since recipes and measures will often be given in what will at first be unfamiliar terms, be *sure* to bring your own measuring spoons and cups. Americans rarely use scales in home cooking. The following measures may be helpful to you as you become accustomed:

In General:

Since a liter is about a *quart,* a half liter is a *pint.*
A *pound* is 500 grams, so think of ½ pound as 250 grams; densities make a difference, however, so a cup of sugar is 200 grams, whereas a cup of flour is only 150!

AMERICAN SPOONS	LIQUID GRAMS	FRENCH MEASURES
1 teaspoon (often written: tsp)	2	1 cuillère à café
1 tablespoon (tbsp)	6	1 cuillère à soupe
		cuillère à bouche
		or: verre à liqueur
6 and ⅔ tbsp	100	1 decilitre
		1 demi-verre
16 tbsp = 1 cup	22	¼ litre (less 2 tbsp)

AMERICAN CUPS	LIQUID GRAMS	FRENCH MEASURES
1 cup = ½ pint	22	½ litre (less 2 tbsp)
2 cups = 1 pint or 1 pound	454	½ litre less ½ decilitre
4 cups = 1 quart	907	⁹⁄₁₀ of a litre
4 quarts = 1 gallon		3.8 litres

or, to put it differently:

1 litre = 4 and ⅓ cups (U.S.A.)
¼ litre = 1 cup plus 1 tbsp
1 decilitre = 6 and ⅔ tbsp
250 grams = ½ pound (U.S.A.)

OVEN SETTINGS MAY BE CONFUSING

AMERICAN OVENS (DEGREES)		CENTIGRADE	FRENCH	BRITISH
140°–250°	Low or "Slow"	70°–121°	"Douce" (#1, #2, #3)	#¼–#1
300°–400°	Moderate	150°–205°	"Moyen" (#5)	#2–#5
400° up	High or "Hot"	205° up	"Vif" (#6 up)	#6 up

CUTS OF MEAT ARE DIFFERENT

There are basic differences in the way meat is cut in different parts of the world. Primarily these differences fall into two methods:

1) The meat is *muscle-boned;* the different muscles are separated;

2) The meat is *unboned;* the retail cuts are sliced across the muscles, bones, and fat.

In the United States, meat is *unboned.* As a result, many cuts have more than one muscle in them, and the degree of tenderness may vary. However, most of the natural fat is left on the meat and because the meat is held on the bones while it is being cooked, there is less shrinkage and added flavor. So there are pluses and minuses to both methods.

One notices the difference most clearly in beef because the animal is so large. Veal, lamb, and pork are butchered in about the same way, however, so a study of the accompanying chart will give you an idea of the way you will find meats cut in this country.

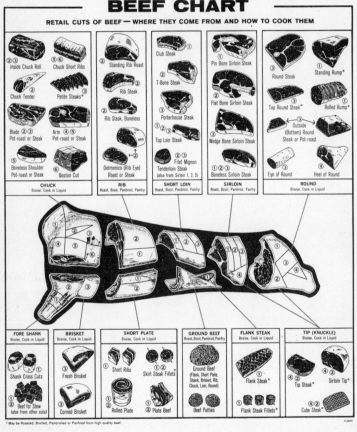

Courtesy of:
National Live Stock and Meat Board
(used with permission)

GRADES AND QUALITIES OF FOODS*

The government is trying to make it easier for shoppers to tell the quality of food before buying it. Grading is carried on by the U.S. Department of Agriculture (abbreviated as USDA). Since it is not required by law that all producers use this service, all foods do not necessarily carry the seal even when the quality is of top level. However, if you learn to recognize and look for the shields, they can help you to know what you are buying. Foods most likely to carry them are beef, veal, lamb, poultry, eggs and butter. (*Note:* The best grade is listed first.)

Beef, Veal, Lamb   U.S. Prime, Choice, Good, Standard

Poultry   U.S. Grades A and B
Watch for the words "Young" or "Broiler" or "Fryer." These all mean the bird is tender. "Mature" means you must cook it in moist heat to tenderize it, or it is likely to be tough.

Eggs   U.S. Grades AA, A, B
Eggs are also classified by size: Extra Large, Large, Medium, and Small. If you see the word "Jumbo," it means biggest of all!

Butter   U.S. Grades AA, A, and B
Grade A is almost as good as AA—the average person cannot tell any difference—and is far cheaper.

Canned, frozen, dried Fruits and Vegetables   1) U.S. Grade A or U.S. Fancy, 2) U.S. Grade B or U.S. Choice, or sometimes Extra Standard, 3) U.S. Grade C or U.S. Standard

Apples   These come under a number of gradations: U.S. Extra Fancy, U.S. Fancy, U.S. No. 1 (note that this is actually the *third* level), U.S. Utility (Good for applesauce, but not for eating uncooked).

---

* (Thanks to the Consumer and Marketing Service of the Department of Agriculture, Washington, D.C.)

Part III

Treaty Agreements on Car Licenses and Registration*

Foreign countries which have signed either the United Nations Convention on Road Traffic or the Inter-American Convention as of 1972:

Albania	Hungary
Algeria	India
Argentina	Ireland
Australia	Israel
Austria	Italy
Barbados	Ivory Coast
Belgium	Jamaica
Botswana	Japan
Bulgaria	Jordan
Cambodia	Laos
Canada	Lebanon
Central African Republic	Luxembourg
Ceylon	Malagasy Republic
Chile	Malawi
China (National Republic)	Malaysia
Congo (Brazzaville)	Mali
Congo (Kinshana)	Malta
Cuba	Mauritius
Cyprus	Monaco
Czechoslovakia	Morocco
Dahomey	Netherlands
Denmark	New Zealand
Dominican Republic	Niger
Ecuador	Norway
Finland	Paraguay
France	Peru
Gambia	Philippines
Ghana	Poland
Greece	Portugal
Guatemala	Rumania
Haiti	Rwanda

* (Information supplied through the courtesy of Miss Joyce M. Wrenn, Assistant Counsel for the Commissioner of Motor Vehicles, New York.)

San Marino
Senegal
Sierra Leone
Singapore
South Africa
Spain
Swaziland
Sweden
Syria
Thailand
Togo
Trinidad-Tobago
Tunisia

Turkey
Uganda
United Arab Republic (Egypt)
United Kingdom (Great Britain)
United States of America
Union of Soviet Socialist Republics
Vatican City
Venezuela
Viet Nam
Western Samoa
Yugoslavia
Zaire (Congo, Kinshasa)
Zambia

INTER-AMERICAN CONVENTION

Brazil	El Salvador	Nicaragua
Colombia	Honduras	Panama
Costa Rica	Mexico	Paraguay

DIRECT RECIPROCITY

Federal Republic of Germany
Mexico
Switzerland

Provisions of both these treaties supersede state laws. They provide that a license or registration issued by any nation which has signed the particular treaty to a resident of the issuing nation will be honored in any other nation which is a signatory to the treaty for a *period of one year* from entry into a particular nation so long as the license or registration remains in effect.

The only action which will affect the validity of such a license is the abandonment by the licensee of his residence in his native country. Such an abandonment of residence will not be presumed to have taken place as long as the person involved is required to return to his native country under the terms of his visa.

In 1968 a new and more comprehensive Convention on Road Traffic was drafted in Vienna at the Conference on Road Traffic. If adopted, this convention will supersede the two treaties listed above.

INDEX

Index

parochial, 144; private, 145–
146; public, 142–144; relation-
ships between parent and, 147–
148; student population, 141;
summer sessions, 149; term,
149–150
Schrafft's Restaurant, 98
Scotch (cocktail), 47
Secondhand bargains, 132–133
Secondhand cars, 74–75
Selective Service, 181
Self-improvement courses, 162
Service stations, 76–77
Shoeshine boys, tipping, 86, 89
Shopping by telephone, 104
Silence, 16–17
Single girls: adult dating, 53–55;
going unescorted, 52–53; paying
for dates, 55; ways to meet men,
55–57
Singles Clubs, 56
Size, geographic, 63–64; climate,
65; and clothes to wear, 65–67;
psychological effect of, 64; time
zones, 64–65
Sizes, clothing (U.S. compared to
European), 187–189
Sizes, food package, 127–128
Ski trips, 170
Slaw (cole slaw), 101
Sleep-overs, 152
Snack bars, 95
So You Want to Import a Pet, 183
Soccer games, 170
Social life: manners and courte-
sies, 40–58; office, 61–62
Speech: bluntness, 16; distance and
bodily contact, 18–19
Speed limit, 78
Sports events, 169–172; arrival and
departure time, 46
Squash (sport), 170
Staff meetings, office, 61

Steady relationship (going steady),
153–154
Student visa, 177
Subway travel, 69, 70–71; avoiding
(after dark), 109
Success, defined, 29
Summer camps, 157
Sunday brunch, 98
Sunday morning coffee hour (after
church), 161
Swimming, 170
Synagogues, 160–161

Tap water, 121
Taxes, 140, 179–180; before leaving the U.S., 180; evasion of,
34; filing dates, 180; household
employees, 140
Taxis, 69–70; complaint about
service, 70; driver rules, 69–70;
fares, 82; metered, 69; sharing
a cab, 69; tipping driver, 86, 87
Tea, ordering, 100
Tea party, arrival and departure
time, 45
Teen-ager activities, 151–159;
clothes and fashions, 152–153;
communes, 155–156; competitive dating, 153; curfew hours
(for girls), 151; dating, 151–
156; going steady, 153–154;
group codes, 152; group dating,
154–156; jobs, 157–159; summer camps, 157; use of drugs,
155
Telegrams and cables, 107–108;
day letter, 108; night letter, 108;
straight, 107
Telephones, 104–107; credit cards,
106; installation, 105; invitations, accepting or regretting,
44; long-distance calls, 106–107;
monthly rates, 105; public, 106;